BEING

GOD

BEING GOD

GOD

Stealing God's Power,
Glory, and
Kingdom

TERRY STUECK

High Plains Bible Mission Publishing
Albuquerque—Atlanta
www.high-plains.org
www.forgiveinstantly.com
www.BeingGod.org

ISBN: 978-0-9961376-4-5

10 9 8 7 6 5 4 3 2   0 5 2 6 1 7

Printed in the United States of America

Unless otherwise noted, all scriptures are taken from the King James Version.

Other scripture versions are notated as follows:
AMP Amplified Bible
BBE Basic Bible in English
CEB Common English Bible
CEV Contemporary English Version
ESV English Standard Version
GNB Good News Bible
GW God's Word
HCSB Holman Christian Standard Version
KJV King James Version
MSG Message Bible
MEV Modern English Version
MKJV Modern King James Version
NET New English Translation
NIV New International Version
NLV New Life Version
NCV New Century Version
NTE New Testament for Everyone
VOICE The Voice Translation
YLT Young's Lateral Translation

∞ This paper meets the requirements of ANSI/NISO Z39.48-1992
(Permanence of Paper)

*Dedicated to those who are continuing to seek
the highest relationship with God in Christ Jesus.*

You don't know
what you don't know

You never discover
what you will not search for

You can't see
what you are blind to

You don't accept
what you don't understand

Matthew 7:7–8

Ask, and it shall be given you; seek, and ye shall find;
knock, and it shall be opened unto you:
For everyone that asketh receiveth;
and he that seeketh findeth;
and to him that knocketh it shall be opened.

Malachi 3:10 (HCSB)

See if I will not open the floodgates of heaven and
pour out a blessing for you without measure.

CONTENTS

# INTRODUCTION

Isaiah 2:11 (GNB)

A day is coming when human pride will be ended
And human arrogance destroyed.
Then the LORD alone will be exalted.

The scriptures declare God the owner of the universe. They also affirm Him as the owner of all the heavens and this planet. The Bible proclaims God owns all the creatures on the earth, including mankind. It also asserts that God owns each individual human life, including you. In other words, God owns everything from the farthest galaxy to the smallest microbe on this earth, and you are in that spectrum.

The problem is we do not acknowledge His ownership. We live as if we owned ourselves. We make our own choices, direct our own affairs, and conduct our lives without considering that there is a powerful God above us who has authority over us. We may believe in Him, ask Him for favors, and even acquiesce to letting Him manage some part of our lives. We may even incorporate truth from scripture into our daily choices that point to His wishes.

Even though we may say, "God is in control" or "I live in the will of God," we have only placed Him in a management-level positon in our life. We want God to take over only when things are going poorly for us. If His solutions are not fast enough, or to our liking, we move Him aside and take over the situation. We do that because we still see the problem as "my" problem. We own the problem because from our point of view, we own ourselves. The words we use reveal our attitude of ownership. We say things like "I have God here to help me" or "Lord, I have a problem." Our terms give us away; "I," "me," and "my" are all ownership words.

We have stolen ownership of our problems from God. If God owns everything, then the problem is His, the outcome is His, and the success or failure of the matter also rests on Him. A more appropriate phrase that reveals His position as owner would be "He solved His problem that happened to involve me."

Thine Is the Kingdom

We have stolen the Garden, this planet. We think we are responsible for it. We think the outcome rests on us because we are responsible. The word "responsible" is an authoritative term. Responsibility rests on the owner. If you think you are responsible, you think you own the item in question. We think we can control this planet, its rain and wind, its temperature and seasons. Are we responsible for fixing these things, or is there a powerful, prevailing God who is the ultimate owner? Can we impede the earthquakes or calm the seas or even stop the volcanoes or the hurricanes? We blame Him for the catastrophes and call them "acts of God," but take responsibility for anything we can exert some control over.

Not only do we think we are responsible for the planet, but we have assumed ownership of our own individual destinies. We consider ourselves owners of the human race and individually, ourselves. We feel responsible for our own success or failure, not taking into account what the creator may have gifted us with or even limited us to. We do not acknowledge He created us and gave us the talent that made the success possible. "My Life" is a popular song by Billy Joel that conveys how we perceive ourselves.

Thine Is the Power

We have stolen God's power. We think we have power to fire God from the management position we elevated Him to. We think He got His promotion from us, that we gave Him something. We perceive that He is grateful and happy that we allow Him such honor.

The fact is just the opposite—God is the owner and can fire us. We can't promote God, nor can we fire Him. We have stolen the owner's power as the final authority. When we steal God's power to hire and fire, we are "being God." He is not the manager we can promote or set aside under our ownership, but rather the owner over us.

Thine Is the Glory

We have stolen His Glory. Every time we elevate ourselves, point to our achievements, or let our pride take us to heights in our minds above reality, we have diminished His glory and taken glory for ourselves.

When an employee invents something, the company is the owner of the invention. They pay the employee to do the work, so they own his time and the inventions he designs. Since God owns us, every good thing we may brag about or try to take glory for is owned by God, who made us and lets us breathe His air. Our pride is the theft of God's glory. We continuously take ownership of all of this, HIS creation.

In the following pages, we will examine the ownership of God and determine His jurisdiction. We will examine how mankind has tried to steal everything God owns. We will look at how that inclination to "Be God" (take His Place as owner) causes us to fail in our understanding of God and who He is. We will look at what life can be when you declare God your owner and live under His authority.

CHAPTER 1

THREE WORDS THAT CHANGED MY LIFE FOREVER

2 Chronicles 7:14

If my people, which are called by my name,

shall humble themselves, and pray . . .

"I asked God."

Those three words changed my life forever. They were the words used to describe a prayer. It was not my prayer, but the prayer of another and the description the man used to convey its meaning that would impact the rest of my days. I heard the prayer on a mountainside high in the Peruvian Andes. I was far into the countryside some four-hour trek from the nearest village helping a missionary, a former classmate in seminary, take the Gospel deep into the land of the Incas to reach a people who had not heard it.

My friend had requested my help with this adventurous task that was far away from his home base in Lima. We shared several characteristics; we were both mission evangelists, dedicated, full of passion, and at times we felt bulletproof. Planning the details of the travel and getting reliable information about the rugged, wild country we were venturing into was difficult to obtain, but a tidal wave far greater than we could resist carried us. We were going there by divine assignment. The farmer's prayer, which he had sent into the heavens, had engulfed our lives and brought us seven thousand miles to his door. Those words changed me and would shadow me for the rest of my days.

So many things had tried to discourage us from making the journey. We recalled some of our more stressful moments sharing the Gospel the previous year pushing the boundaries on the Napo River, an Amazon tributary. As we drew close to Ecuador in our makeshift houseboat, communication became difficult as we began to encounter unknown Indian dialects.

A week before my departure, an earthquake in Peru had devastated a village of six thousand people. The news came over the wire that all the houses of the entire village slid down the side of a mountain, leaving only two survivors. Where was God taking us, and what purpose would be served by going to another dangerous place?

I had traveled three days by car to Miami. The South American turbo prop based out of Ecuador delayed the departure for repairs so it could survive the flight. The direct, nonstop jet to Lima was more than I could afford. I had a ticket on a hopscotch flight landing in Caracas, Bogotá, and Quito before arriving in the cloud-covered city of Lima. Upon landing, I boarded an old,

American school bus that had been sold to a South American bus line. The bus company had painted it wild blue and lettered it with advertisements of all kinds. They had moved the seats closer together to accommodate shorter people and get more passengers aboard.

The bus traveled south on the Pan-American Highway to Nazca where it made a left into the rugged gravel roads of the Andes mountains. For thirty-six hours, with very few stops, the bus ground through mountain-cliff roads on its way to Coracora. As I looked out over the edge of the road, there were old, burned-out hulks of buses that had fallen from the overhanging mountain walls to their doom. I expanded my prayer life with short prayers for safety mingled with questions about the future. God's ownership of His servant was being tried by fire. Could I walk into the furnace with Shadrach, Meshach, and Abednego, or would someone have to throw me in? My owner had determined I should go, so I was on my way.

At a small village named Puquio, the bus stopped to pick up a passenger. The driver had not intended to linger, but the passengers swarmed the doors to exit, as many had been shouting for a pit stop for the last couple of hours. We picked up a second driver to act as a spotter on the rugged mountain roads ahead. We also picked up a very drunk hombre who smelled like he had fallen in the tank at the brewery. There was only one seat left, and it was beside me. I was the tallest one on the bus, so the empty seat had given me a little room for my knees as I sat angled in the seat. But the inebriated man eliminated that option, so I sat straight up to accommodate the new rider. I let him sit next to the window so I could put one knee into the aisle for some relief.

The next hundred miles took ten hours to travel. It was one-lane, mountain gravel with tight turns requiring the driver to reverse and zigzag his back wheels closer to the mountain to avoid tumbling over the side. The spotter often walked ahead of us guiding the driver and watching the outside wheel. I would have gladly traded places with him.

About an hour out of Puquio, the man beside me shouted that he needed a pit stop. The driver did not answer. Nor did he answer the second or third requests. In urgent need, the man took off his sombrero and relieved himself in it. He put the hat out the window, turned it over to dump it, brought it back in, and placed it back on his head. I grew up on a farm and knew life from the raw side, but this trip taught me a whole new set of tricks.

The name Coracora is a Spanish version of the Quechua Indian name Qura Qura, meaning a collection of special herbal plants. It had caught the attention of my missionary friend in Lima who saw an advertisement for the village festival to celebrate the three-hundred-year anniversary of their god's physical appearance. The advertisement had appeared a year in advance of the ten-day festival. It had given my friend enough time to contact me for help and to make all the arrangements for the journey. He wanted to use the gathering in Coracora as an opportunity to take the Gospel to a village that to his knowledge had never been visited by a missionary.

It was the mid-1970s. There were no phones in the mountains, only shortwave radio into our intended destination. It was not a tourist area or place to take your family, but rather a hotbed of civil strife as communist rebel groups tried to incite Inca Indian uprisings against the democratic governments of Bolivia and Peru.

All roads were desert gravel, made of the rock and sand they were carved through. There were occasional wide spots in case you met another oncoming vehicle. One vehicle would back up depending on which driver was willing. Drivers were armed to protect from highwaymen, but the general population was too poor to own guns. All the buses were old school buses from the States. They made a colorful picture as they passed one another on the roads all painted in different exotic colors. In open flats on some of the mountain plateaus, they would leave the road and race two and three abreast, taking a shortcut across the desert plains trying to beat each other to the next canyon where the road again narrowed to one lane. We had found the last remnants of the Wild West. And it was just as rough, rugged, and dusty as the old Western movies had portrayed it.

During the festival in Coracora, the population swelled because the people who had moved away returned for a visit and all the area farmers from fifty miles around came to sell and celebrate. We were going to evangelize on the streets and hand out Gospel tracts printed in Spanish and Quechua. We would use street corners, plazas, or parks to have small gatherings as well.

Arrival in Coracora

To our surprise, we found a church in Coracora. It was a small storefront with a sign lettered in Spanish and Quechua. We had no idea that Christians had ever visited the village before. There had been no reports from the area of Christian efforts. We inquired as to where we might find the person with a key since the front door had a master padlock on the latch. We found a neighboring shopkeeper who told us a farmer four hours out of the village had the key as he pointed down a street toward a trail out of the village. It was not a road, but more of a rocky footpath clinging to the slopes. The man drew a crude map to the farmer's house for us.

The farmer was reported to be the only one they knew who had ever been at the church. The neighbor storekeeper did not know of any other people who ever went into the church. He reported the farmer had traveled to Lima where he had been influenced by a missionary. The farmer had rented the store and was inviting people to come and study the Bible. We were in awe that God may have already provided a place for a service and privacy off the streets to talk with the residents and pray. But more importantly, He had provided a dedicated follower as a starting point.

We found a hotel in the village. It was the high-class hotel where the famous matadors from Spain who had come for the bullfight were staying. We were in the best the village had to offer. It cost us four soles, the Peruvian dollar. That was about twenty cents at that time in our exchange. The door had a latch with a padlock. I had padlocks at home as a boy just like it. I got them out of gum-machine dispensers for five cents. They were as big as my thumb and about as strong.

There was a table and one chair in the room. The rest of the concrete floor was available for you to throw your sleeping bag anywhere you wanted. Travel advice for Peru in the seventies— bring a sleeping bag and make sure it was a warm one. Even though the temperatures would hit seventy during the day because of the high sun and little air to filter it, the mountain nights would freeze at that altitude.

The bathroom . . . did I mention a bathroom? It was an open area in the center courtyard surrounded by the rooms. They had built a knee wall around it so the actual commode was not visible from three sides, but the toilet had been broken and was cemented back together with concrete surrounding the bowl. We crashed for twelve hours of sleep. The altitude adjustment to sixteen thousand feet and thirty-six sleepless hours on the bus had taken its toll.

The Mountain Farm

We started in the morning on our four-hour expedition. Up and down steep mountain trails, rocky terrain, and all at sixteen thousand feet, we finally arrived at the farmstead. There were two buildings there set in an L shape. The first was a one-room, one-story adobe mud house with thatched roof. The other building was similar but about double the length with barn doors open and a pig or two milling near it. Chickens roamed the area and paid no attention to us as we approached.

We introduced ourselves to the farmer and explained to him what we had come to do. There was silence for a moment. Tears began to well in his eyes. He took a moment to gain a form of composure and said, "I asked God to send someone to help me." There they were, the three words that would captivate me for eternity: "I ASKED GOD." With those words, the power of the universe was unleashed onto the world stage.

How profound! I was an answer to someone's prayer! Hearing that statement after such a long journey changed my life forever. Never again would I doubt God's power and ability. When you become the answer to a prayer, you no longer belong to yourself. You are owned and directed by the God of this universe, who will put you where He needs you.

God can take a Phillip (Acts 8:26) and direct him into the desert where he leads an Ethiopian to Jesus before he is spirited away to another needy person. He can take a Daniel from the lion's den and put him in the king's court (Daniel 6:22). He can take a Nehemiah and stand him on the walls of Jerusalem (Nehemiah 6:3). He can take a Gideon with three hundred men and destroy a mighty army (Judges 7:22). He can pull Shadrach, Meshach, and Abednego from the fiery furnace and put them in a king's palace (Daniel 3:28–30). He is the God who can take Jonah from the belly of a whale and have him preaching in the streets of Nineveh to bring an entire city to repentance (Jonah 3:1–5).

He is the God who can place me any day, at any time, exactly where He wants me. I revel at the times He has used me to answer the prayers of others. If you respect God's role as the owner of your life, you will live out the words of Psalm 37:23: "The steps of a good man are ordered by the LORD."

Has my life been easy, or without trial and tribulation? Certainly not! But through it all, I have learned to trust in Him. I learned that having Him be the owner was a far better outcome than anything I could engineer or design. I learned to look around to see who had prayed for help. I learned that God has no accidents. Nothing was incidental; God had a purpose for my steps.

God can take you to the side entrance of the prayers of others and plant you in the middle of their answer. He uses those who belong to Him. He lets those who own themselves wander in the wilderness until they find what they are looking for. What are you looking for? Be careful, lest you find the wrong thing. "Seek first the kingdom of God," writes Matthew in Matthew 6:33. Seek to have Him be your owner; He will use you mightily for the pulling down of strongholds (2 Corinthians 10:4).

Leaving Coracora

The farmer opened the church for those ten days and worked alongside us in the streets. We gave out invitations during the day and held services every night. When we left Coracora, the church had eight committed souls added to it and another dozen interested seekers. They agreed to meet every week. My friend agreed to visit them once a month to encourage them.

We left Coracora on a different bus line and traveled south over plateaus and mesas, taking the passes and running along streams to avoid the hard mountain roads. The travel was at a higher speed, but longer. We arrived at the Pacific coast two hundred miles south of Nazca at the fishing village of Atico. The bus stopped at an isolated oceanside restaurant where we enjoyed our first steak-and-eggs breakfast since leaving the States. We rejoiced over what God had accomplished in us and through us.

Nostalgia

Out of nostalgia, I recently returned to the Andes by way of Google Maps and Street View. It is amazing to be able to travel the very roads we took so many years ago via computer and three-sixty photography shot from a Google car. Now, the road from Nazca to Puquio is two lanes and paved. I could see tourist buses on the roads, as Machu Picchu and other Inca ruins in the area were declared historical sites in the eighties. I could see a single telephone line running near the road, indicating new inventions had arrived in the land of the Incas.

The villages have not changed, nor could I detect any noticeable lifestyle changes. But there were no pictures on Google Maps of the cliffhanging road from Puquio to Coracora. There is no way to widen a road that overhangs the cliff edges. No paving machine could make the corners to negotiate the hundred miles. Even the owner of the Google car had declined to make that journey and photograph its treachery.

Ephesians 3:8–9

Unto me, who am less than the least of all saints,
is this grace given,
that I should preach among the Gentiles
the unsearchable riches of Christ;
And to make all men see
what is the fellowship of the mystery,
which from the beginning of the world
hath been hid in God,
who created all things by Jesus Christ . . .

Philippians 1:21

For to me to live is Christ, and to die is gain.

CHAPTER 2

OWNERSHIP

Malachi 3:8 (VOICE)

"Will someone steal from God?"
Yet you are *always* stealing from Me!
But you *self-centered people still* ask,
"How have we stolen from You?"

Have you ever owned something you wish you hadn't? As owner, you're responsible for all the repair expenses, upkeep, maintenance, management, legal requirements, and disposal. As an owner, the burden to care for the item, or hire and pay someone else to do it for you, falls squarely on your shoulders. Either way, you pay.

You also reap any benefits of ownership. Owning a business can be an excellent source of income, but it also requires a piece of your life since you are responsible for it and its success. Business owners often work eighty hours a week, often worrying and fretting at night rather than sleeping. Being the owner puts you in charge of the business's success and failure. You are responsible for the accounts payable and receivable. Collecting the accounts can be a far greater burden than paying the bills. If either task goes awry, a business failure is not far off.

Have you ever taken ownership of something that belonged to God? If you are uncertain what God is supposed to own, that may be a tough question. In the next few chapters, we will explore what belongs to God. We will examine the expanse of His ownership. We will consider times when we have taken ownership of issues that really belonged to God. By taking ownership of His property, authority, and glory, we assumed responsibility for things beyond our capabilities.

The First and Last Day in the Life of a Boat Owner

I was ecstatic about buying my first ski boat. It was a twenty-three-foot inboard cabin cruiser. We had teenage children who yearned to ski. The boat was an exciting craft with canvas-covered aft and pilot helm. Imagine: a country guy from the western prairie had achieved enough success to blow that much money on a toy and feel good about it. I became a boat owner, or had I become a slave to the boat?

We docked the boat at a marina. There was a monthly rental fee for the covered parking slip where we could keep the boat tied up when it was not in use. The one-hundred-gallon gas tank had a limited number of marinas to supply the fuel, all having a limited number of customers, so they charged a heavy duty for a gallon of gas. It took a huge bite in the wallet to fill the tank compared to filling my car. The resistance plowing through water and the load of skiers made the 350-horse inboard motor empty the fuel tank in just a few hours.

Are you getting the picture? Not only did you need a good reserve of cash to buy it, but it was going to be a continual drain on the budget just to keep it. Next, we needed a tandem trailer to move it to other lakes. The insurance bill also came to my desk. Having it serviced was a major expense, and any repairs were high because they required specialty work. Boats are considered luxury items, which engender luxury prices for all the surrounding services they require.

The money was only one liability. The boat had to be cleaned. The underside turned green from being left in the water. The canvas and topside turned black from the mold and required more energy and time. Packing and unpacking for each outing was an ordeal. The number of toys and skis to pull grew larger.

We used the boat to take the children through those early teen years before they got their driver's licenses, but once the independence of driving landed on their shoulders, the lake no longer had the pull that it once had. Once the children's attention had moved on, I sold the boat as fast as I could. The day I sold it, I was just as happy as I had been the day I purchased it. I am glad I had the boat, but it taught me a lesson about the heavy duties of ownership.

The First and Last Day as Owner of the Planet

We need to examine the mess we have made of our lives because we did not let the creator maintain ownership of things that belonged to Him. The scriptures will lay out our journey to discover the most basic premise of the Bible that is hidden from most people. The greatest secret in the universe unfolds in this big adventure ahead. The nature of our human passion to "own" has blinded us so that we are unable to see what God proclaims on nearly every page of the Bible; God is still the owner.

Maybe we tried to take ownership of the Garden that was owned by God because it was there to take. Just as the lake was there calling for me to get a boat, so Adam in the Garden saw and took. When he became the rule-maker of the Garden, he replaced God as the rightful authority. Adam became the owner of something that would bring pain and destruction in his life and relationships. Every time we take ownership of something that belongs to God, we are being God. We tread across a forbidden line by trying to take His place as the rightful owner. We bring upon ourselves unwanted consequences that bring regrets far beyond any gain we may have intended to receive.

My journey into the discovery of God's powerful position as owner started with just a simple step. In the process of learning to be forgiving, I canceled my ownership of the debts the offenders owed me. In so doing, I had unknowingly transferred ownership of those offenses to God. Just because I forgave and was not going to collect from those offenders did not mean God would not pursue the collection. In making the gigantic step of becoming a forgiving person, I had stumbled on the truth of His ownership.

When His ownership became a focus of my thoughts, I connected with instant forgiveness, the capability to let God retain ownership of a situation and avoid taking offense. This monumental shift in my thinking kept me from relapsing every time a new offense occurred.

I had just taken the first step in liquidating my assets on this planet. On the day I gave up owning those assets, my joy was greater than in all the days I had in possession of them.

Jeremiah 17:9–10

The heart is deceitful above all things,

and desperately wicked: who can know it?

I the LORD search the heart, I try the reins . . .

Proverbs 4:23

Keep thy heart with all diligence;

for out of it are the issues of life.

CHAPTER 3

BURNOUT AND MIDLIFE CRISIS

Matthew 11:28–30

Come unto me, all ye that labour and are heavy laden,

and I will give you rest.

Take my yoke upon you, and learn of me;

for I am meek and lowly in heart:

and ye shall find rest unto your souls.

For my yoke is easy, and my burden is light.

In the summers on the prairie of Iowa and eastern Nebraska in the late 1940s and early '50s, farmers joined forces to work together in the haymaking process. Family farms of four families per square mile dotted the prairie. The average farm was 160 acres, with a square mile being 640 acres. Making hay was a very labor-intensive task with the pressure of unpredictable weather being a driving force. From cutting to stacking in a barn, any rain on the crop caused it to mold and be ruined. Once it was cut down, the pressure was on to dry it, bale it, stack it, and store it before any rain occurred.

The farms were small at that time because of the labor it took to care for a certain-size farm. Born in the mid-1940s, I was a young boy when a great transition in the farming industry occurred. Tractors had been invented and reinvented to the point they became practical and available to the average farmer.

Horses were the standard laborsaving devices up to that time; now, machines replaced them. The transition was fairly rapid. One of the farmers in the area purchased a tractor, which became part of the haymaking process that year. The eyes of the other farmers widened as the new tractor outworked the old standard-bearer, the horse. Over the course of the next five years, the horses disappeared from one farm at a time until only tractors remained.

Now, instead of six farmers joining together, only three were needed. The work was faster and the rains less of a problem because of the new speed. Over the course of the past six decades, the tractors and machines to help with the work have transformed farming from a hundred acres per farmer to thousands of acres that one farmer can handle. Now, only one farmer lives on several square miles.

Yoke

The word "yoke" was a common term until the tractor age. Before all our gas-powered tools, teams of oxen or horses worked farms. A yoke was the wooden cross member that attached to two collars that rested on the animals' necks. The yoke not only joined two animals together so they could pull equally, but also secured the animals to a drawbar attached to a working device like a plow, wagon, harrow, or log.

Yoked together, both animals carried an equal burden. No matter the difference in strength or size, both had to pull equally to keep the yoke even and not bind on their necks. If one animal slacked off, the other matched that same slack so the yoke stayed even. As a team got used to each other, they got better at pulling their own weight at the right time and cooperating with their teammate. The expectation was that the work would be shared equally.

When all the horses yoked together did what was directed by the driver, the owner of the team, everything went well. When one or more horses did not pull equally, the work suffered. The key to a successful yoke of oxen or horses was the owner's oversight— he had to keep them equally yoked. It was not wise to yoke two animals that were too different in size, strength, or temperament.

It was also important to have enough animals of the right size to do the task without straining or hurting the teams. If you were taking a team of horses into the woods to pull a log that weighed three thousand pounds and you only had two horses in the yoke, each weighing one thousand pounds, they would have to work hard to drag the log that outweighed them. The smart owner would get his bigger horses that weighed two thousand pounds each, or put four one-thousand-pound horses together as a double team to drag the three-thousand-pound log. That would make the work easy.

The Burden Is His

Jesus calls to those who are laboring hard and failing under the weight of the load they are burdened with. They may feel they are pulling the load alone without help. We are alone in our bodies and minds. No one lives in this body or looks out the windows of my eyes except me. We are alone as God noticed in the Garden; Genesis 2:18 will enlighten us: "And the LORD said, It is not good that the man should be alone." Despite people and family all around, you are alone in your body. Only you live with your thoughts and self-image. God created Eve as a mate, not a solution. She lives beside a man as an equal yoked next to him; she does not cohabitate inside a man's skin.

> We're all sentenced to solitary confinement inside
> our own skins, for life.
>
> **—Tennessee Williams**

We spend our entire lives alone in our own body. No one sees the world through your eyes except you. No one has the same experiences and thought or knows what is going on inside you but you. Only God can know the real you.

Psalm 139:1–2

O LORD, thou hast searched me, and known me.
Thou knowest my downsitting and mine uprising,
thou understandest my thought afar off.

Burnout at work and a midlife crisis occur when we think we are doing all the work without the help of a team member. They result from being alone in your own skin, trapped in your own thoughts and opinions, feeling as though there is no help or way to accomplish the grand goal of perfectionism. You feel like you are carrying the weight of the world with no help in sight.

In his grand adventure to take God's place as owner of the Garden, Adam passed down the flaw that caused this predicament. Like him, we make the mistake of taking ownership and see ourselves as the driver of the team, the owner. We don't see that we are to be yoked in a team under the direction of God, the true owner. We fail, burn out, and crash on the basis that we had this tremendous load to bear that was greater than we could handle. We made the human mistake of attaching to a load that was not made for man to bear. God never created us to own the Garden, the universe, or ourselves.

When we think we own everything, we feel responsible for everything. We think we are the driver of the team instead of being a member of the team. As we projected our ownership over everything, we have assumed responsibility and taken on the weight of the world. We have moved out from under the yoke and assumed the driver's position. We think we own a team and are responsible for the work of the day. We have a flare-out because we are "being God," taking on things that belong to God.

Jesus says, "Take my yoke upon you." Jesus owns the yoke. He is not going to share it with you and carry the other half of the yoke, but rather He is the driver who will pair you with an equal. Erroneously, we think that Jesus will pull half our loads, as our equal. A popular slogan of our time that conveys our lofty view of ourselves is "God is my copilot." We always put ourselves too high on the totem pole, somewhere equal to or above God. We take the reins instead of the yoke—assuming the responsibility that belongs to God—and that move spells our downfall.

Sorry, Jesus is the team driver; He is not under the yoke with you. He is the owner of the task, the team, and the wagon. The team has no responsibility other than to pull.

The Yoke of Expectations

When Jesus asks us to take his yoke upon us, He is not going to put us on a bigger task than we can handle. We can trust Him not to set us up for failure. He asks us to accept His expectations of service—to work together with others as part of a team. The higher we regard and follow the owner's direction, the easier the task will be. Moving God from a position under the yoke (comanager) to that of a driver (owner) is the big attitude change that makes shouldering the yoke easy.

The yoke's change in ownership changes the expectations. How would you compare the expectations you place on yourself to those God expects of you? If you put heavy expectations on yourself assuming ownership, you will be disappointed, dejected, or even depressed by your failure to meet those expectations. If you assume the driver's place, you will suffer burnout and a midlife crisis because you have taken on God's position. Your expectation of others is incorrect and misguided. You put undue stress on those around you by holding them to the exalted position you have elevated yourself to. You will lose because GOD'S SHOES are hard to fill.

The Burden Is Light

News flash! Your spouse is not your servant. You are both servants of the grand owner of the universe, God. You are teammates. Teammates don't balk or pull apart; they pull together.

News nugget! Your employees are not your servants. You are co-laborers who are stronger under the same yoke—armed with different talents, but meant to pull together. If you make your employees feel like they share the task, they will pull with you.

Jesus says take HIS yoke, make Him your God and owner. When He is owner, the expectations are on Him and not you. You are just there for the help you can give Him. If the task fails or succeeds, it is all His responsibility.

Under God's ownership, the burden is light because He manages the needs of the task against the abilities of the teams. When we assume ownership and take the reins, the burden is impossible as we place our misguided expectations on others we deem as being under our yoke. We suffer burnout and midlife crises because we are "being God" by taking the wrong positon as owner rather than co-laborers under the God who knows us better than we know ourselves.

CHAPTER 4

LIVING UNDER
HIS OWNERSHIP

Galatians 2:20 (GNB)

[S]o that it is no longer I who live,
but it is Christ who lives in me.
This life that I live now,
I live by faith in the Son of God,
who loved me and gave his life for me.

Back in the Real World

Thirty years had passed since I had, in anger, intentionally rammed another car with my Cadillac on the streets of Chicago. Now, I faced another antagonistic driver in Atlanta. I sat at a stoplight as the lead car in the left lane, needing to make a right-hand turn in a quarter mile to enter an interstate ramp. As I waited for the light to turn green, I surmised I could switch a lane to the right if the big engine in my pickup could beat the car next to me. If they hesitated even for a moment or drove at a normal pace, I could make the lane change without a drastic acceleration. The best plan was to hit the gas the moment the green light appeared.

The light-blue car next to me also hit the gas with gusto. I backed off immediately so he could go ahead and I could pull in behind him in the large space we had just created from the next tier of cars behind us. That didn't work. The car beside me slowed to stay even with me. I punched it again. That didn't work either. The driver's actions mirrored mine. I braked hard to let him go ahead, but he did the same to stay beside me. He was determined to not give me a space to change lanes.

Southern drivers are usually the most courteous and considerate drivers I have ever known. They are polite and generous. Many times I have appreciated the grace and mercy they have shown. I learned to give that treatment back to them and extend patience for other driving styles.

But the enormous change that occurred in my life since the Chicago incident was the result of becoming a forgiving person. Between these two driving events, I had drained my heart of all the bitter feelings from my childhood. I had learned to handle current incidents by forgiving and letting God retain ownership of those events. And I was in the final editing stages of writing *Forgive Instantly & Live Free* as a helpful guide for others learning to master forgiveness.

So this time, my reactions were different. The other driver was in a competitive mood. I had lost that contentious spirit in my driving, along with other unacceptable attitudes, because I'd given ownership of my life back to God. The lesson to forgive and to be able to do it instantly is a life change of monumental proportions. My attitude now was one of peace and calm.

The other driver was having a bad day, or maybe it was a good day if he was a person looking for a challenge. But I was just trying to merge onto the interstate in peace. I was not angered or disturbed. I was going to have to find a sane way to deal with him that would diffuse the tension and not add fuel to the fire that burned in him. The opposing car had dark windows, which blocked any possibility of seeing the driver.

I stopped all efforts to speed up and continued to slow down in my lane, waiting for him to proceed so I could change lanes. We both came to a dead stop right at the ramp entrance. The ramp curving away from traffic created a dead space marked out with white hash lines. I ended up sitting in that excess area of painted-out roadway. The traffic behind me could continue while I had a neutral area to stop and wait. As soon as the car behind the competitive driver closed the gap and came to a stop behind him, it blew its horn for the antagonistic driver to move. That did the trick. He made a sharp turn onto the ramp leading to the interstate. My turn signal had been on the entire time, so the cars behind him let me make the turn onto the ramp. You would have thought the event was over.

I slowly accelerated to stay well behind the hot rod who was in front of me clogging the ramp. When we entered the traffic lane of the interstate I was at least five car lengths behind him, staying back intentionally. He stayed well below the speed limit, goading me to try to pass him. He had been unsuccessful at preventing me from turning, so he was not finished venting his animosity.

My life is so different now and I enjoy living in peace. I stayed well behind the man with lots of space to not show any aggression toward him. We were well below the speed limit for almost a mile before he gave up and went speeding on his way.

Never did I feel or show anger during the incident. There was no attempt to make hand gestures or fists in the air on my part. I could not give you any idea of what was going on in the other car with dark, tinted windows. To me, it was just a car. It was just all in a day's events that can occur to almost anyone. Rather than having hard feelings, I smiled at my wife, who was with me. She did comment about the joy of experiencing another road confrontation. She too has made a remarkable journey into the forgiving lifestyle.

"Let's pray for the man in the other car so he doesn't have an accident. God may put him to the test today for his attitude," we said. When God is your owner, it is easy to fulfill simple requests Jesus made, like praying for those who persecute you. The other driver's offenses directed at me were charged to God, my owner. If God wants to collect, it is up to Him. He can and will take care of His own property. I can rest in His care.

I have learned a truth that changed who I am and how I live my life. I learned not to step in and take ownership of something that belongs to God. He owns me and will take care of me. I do not have to beat anyone or get even for their apparent inflictions. But also, God owns the other person, whether he is a good or bad person. God will dole out to them whatever they need and will do so as He sees fit to teach, correct, or care for those He owns. I have learned to forgive instantly, but better yet, not to even take offense or own the issue at all. Let God solve it. He loves being God.

A Lasting Change

Before this event ever happened, I had won the battle of a lifetime. I had conquered anger and animosity against others by learning to unconditionally forgive all those in my past who had offended and harmed me. But I had gone further. I had learned the secret of instant forgiveness. I had learned the ownership principle that is hidden on nearly every page of the Bible.

I had learned not to step in front of God and stand in for what He had promised to do. I had learned not to own the things that belong to God. I had learned to stop being God.

Because of our very nature that was born in us, we find it difficult to understand the most basic principle in the Bible. In thirty years of church attendance, I never heard a single message on God's ownership. In seminary, it was never discussed. I pulled out my systematic theology textbooks from college—no mention of ownership. It is a subject out of sight and off the radar. It is though we are blind to it. Right in front of our eyes, we still gaze over it without comprehending the depth of what it means.

Coming to this subject of God's ownership and letting Him own the things that belong to Him, I had made an incredible journey to let him own the first thing many of us are unwilling to sign over to His ownership. There is one thing we can easily learn to give back to God if we can find willingness in our heart—our baggage from the past. Keeping ownership of it is harming us. Forgiving by cancelling the debt and turning it over to God will set us free.

Philippians 3:12 (CEV)

I have not yet reached my goal,
and I am not perfect.
But Christ has taken hold of me.

CHAPTER 5

BIRD'S-EYE VIEW

Isaiah 55:9

For as the heavens are higher than the earth,

so are my ways higher than your ways,

and my thoughts than your thoughts.

Lost in the Forest

When I moved to Georgia, it was the first time I had ever lived in a forest. I had spent my entire life on the open prairie of Iowa. The farmstead I grew up on sat on one of the rolling hilltops of Iowa. From that vantage point, you could see ten miles in every direction.

When I moved to Georgia, it was a severe culture shock. It was not a problem with the people—they were warm and friendly. Trees were the problem—they were everywhere. The roads in

Georgia had been built on the Indian trails that ran the ridgelines and valleys of foothills of the Appalachian Mountains. Not a single road was straight. With trees lining the side of the roads and a continuous curve, you could not see more than a quarter mile ahead. Trees hung over the roads and blocked out the sky. Within a week, I had claustrophobia so bad I was ready to pack up and leave.

My Georgia friends will say I am exaggerating; it's not that bad. I would agree, it's not that bad *when you get used to it*. It is so different not being able to see a great distance nor be able to get your bearings from visible landmarks. I felt lost every day, all day long. It was an unsettling feeling.

I found relief by visiting one of the two mountains near Atlanta. My favorite was Stone Mountain, even though Kennesaw Mountain was closer. Stone Mountain is a bald chunk of granite standing a thousand feet in the air with no trees on it. From the top, you can see a hundred miles. It was like medicine to my soul. I would go and spend hours soaking in the sun and enjoying the view. Without its reprieve, I may never have survived the transition from a prairie dog to forest squirrel. I had never been fenced in before, so the adjustment was severe.

Lost in the Scriptures

Our Christian life has some similarities. We are often lost in the details of a chapter or even a single verse. We cover the lives of the historical figures. We are always in a text or chapter and seldom get a grand view of the entire Bible from beginning to end from a high place. We are often lost in verses or even a doctrine and fail to see the overall picture from afar.

I found a whole new perspective of the Bible when I climbed the mountain of forgiveness. From that vantage point, I could see for miles and miles. I discovered off in the distance, God had been the owner and creator. Standing tall at the beginning of creation was a maker declaring Himself the owner. In the other direction, God created a new heaven and a new earth, and again, He was the sole owner. And from the mountaintop, drawing in closer from those two faraway points, it was clear that God had not given up his ownership. Just because Lucifer and man make claim to it and pretend to own it does not mean they have succeeded. They are in a continuous fight to steal what is God's. The devil and mankind both want to be God or equal to Him. They don't understand that only one God can exist; only one can be called "eternal." There can be no equal to God; it's impossible. We get stuck in doctrines and issues and miss the big picture of the underlying battle for real ownership, the foundation of sin, the desire to be God.

Adam and Eve failed to steal the Garden—they only succeeded in being evicted and moved to the wastelands of this earth. It is from those wastelands we are lost in the forest of our own making, not able to see the big picture of what is going on with this war over ownership between man and God.

Thank God He loves us and has not given up on us totally. He is redemptive; we are not cast away forever, but have an opportunity to accept His invitation and provision to return by way of Jesus. He has not declared war on us as we have on Him. He gives His favor to us in John 3:16 with these words: "For God so loved the world, that HE GAVE His only begotten Son, that whosoever believeth in HIM should not perish, but have everlasting life."

CHAPTER 6

THE VIEW FROM HEAVEN

Lamentations 1:12

Is it nothing to you, all ye that pass by?

behold, and see if there be any sorrow like unto my

sorrow,

which is done unto me,

wherewith the LORD hath afflicted me in the day

of his fierce anger.

The Christian song "I'll Walk with God" certainly has a good message and a high aspiration for a person to achieve. But walking *with* God is not the same as walking *as* God, or expressed another way, walking in His shoes. We hear about Adam and Eve, what they said, how they felt, what they did, but what about God? Can you walk in God's shoes and see what He sees? What happened to God in the Garden of Eden at the time of the fall of Adam and Eve? How did God feel at the rebellion of His own creation, knowing it would require Jesus's death to redeem them? How did He see the events that have brought us to where we are now? Can we find an example in our lives of something similar that would reveal His point of view?

I Was Robbed

It was a little late in the evening to stop for a motel. In my traveling ministry, I usually tried to make it all the way home without another layover. After having been away for a couple weeks, sleeping in host homes or hotels, I was always ready for the shelter of my home. I would try to drive the distance without taking another night in a faraway place.

But this night's travel was too much to bear. After a week in Wausau and another in Green Bay, I had spoken twice that day, packed, and headed home to Des Moines. I was doing fine as I passed through Milwaukee. At Racine, I began to nod a bit behind the wheel. By the time I reached the northern suburbs of Chicago, I could not go on. So I pulled into a motel along the interstate and got a room for the night. I did not need to carry a lot of baggage in with me since I would be up early and back on the road for home.

The light of day woke me as the sun brightened the room, shining on the drawn curtains. I made coffee, showered, and dressed. Within thirty minutes, I was ready to lock up and head out with the only bag I had bothered to bring in with me. I stepped out the door to my car to an unwelcome surprise. My car had been broken into.

In those days, before cell phones, I traveled with a CB radio. It was missing. My bags had been rifled through. My camera and audiovisual equipment were gone. I had been robbed while I slept. They had not taken my Bible. Little did they know it was the most valuable thing I had.

A Bible can be replaced at a nominal cost, but not this one. I often bought hardcover Bibles because they were inexpensive and easy to give away to people I met and ministered to. But the one left in my car that evening was my wide-margin Bible that I had all my sermon outlines inscribed into the margins of. It contained my life's work in the ministry up to that time, so I had something to be thankful for. I had my Bible.

I did not call the police or even tell the motel management. The value of the things taken could all be replaced below the cost of the deductible on my insurance. I had another eight hours on the road to get home, so taking time in Chicago with a police report that would likely not result in a positive outcome was not an option. I had lost some things I owned, but that was not the loss that most concerned me. Something far worse had been taken from me.

I had been damaged emotionally. It was internal loss that hurt far more than the external things that were missing. I felt angry, insulted, disrespected, violated, and depressed. There was shock and disbelief, at times denial, and sadness. But the wound was deeper. I now had a fear and lack of trust in the sanctity of my things as well as a doubt about my own safety. The damage to my person was far greater than the damage to my things. And this was just my car. How much greater is the feeling of being violated to those whose homes have been invaded?

Can You Feel What God Feels?

We cannot know for certain God's feelings about what happened in the Garden of Eden with the loss God suffered of trust and bond between Him and Adam. But maybe we can get a glimpse of His feelings by comparing our feelings when something we own is violated and taken from us. We are so self-centered to have never stopped to try to examine how God must have felt. Our attention has always been directed at Adam and Eve, not God.

God's Garden was under threat because one of His creatures was replacing Him as the rule-maker. His Garden had been violated; His untouchable tree had been touched and eaten of. But not only the Garden, His prize creature had fallen into moral decay and now saw himself as naked and afraid. So God lost the sanctity of the Garden and the fellowship of His creature that He had made in His own image. We can put a price on all these items and inventory His loss, but there is more . . .

There was far more than the Garden at stake. He must have felt a personal attack on Himself. He suffered a personal loss. This was not just an attack on His property, the Garden, and the creatures in it. It was an attack on Him. He may have felt insulted, diminished, belittled, disrespected, and robbed of His status as the owner of the universe. His creature that He made for His happiness and good pleasure was now out for its own pleasure only. He may have felt ignored and questioned, unvalued, and cast aside.

His prized creature had just tried to take His place as rule-maker, a personal insult. Adam tried to be God. The loss to God was not the Garden, but the emotional tie that He lost with Adam and Eve, who had walked with Him in the cool of the day near the stream. For God did not lose the Garden, Adam did. Adam's attempt to take over the Garden only resulted in his eviction. We live in the wilderness, a place God banished us to, where we can go practice our attempts at ownership.

The entire journey of man from that point on has been a miscarriage of direction. We have continued down a path to own everything we touch, including ourselves. Adam should have apologized, admitted his mistake, and given the core of the apple back to God. But instead, he kept the core and passed out excuses with no repentance. Our first father, Adam, failed at every turn. Do you think any of us could do much better?

Can you walk in God's shoes?
Can you see what God sees?
Can you feel what God feels?
Can you know what God knows?

CHAPTER 7

NEW TESTAMENT PROMISED LAND—THE PLACE OF REST

Hebrews 4:8–11

For if Jesus had given them rest,

then would he not afterward have spoken of

another day.

There remaineth therefore a rest to the people of God.

For he that is entered into his rest, he also hath

ceased from his own works, as God did from his.

Let us labour therefore to enter into that rest,

lest any man fall after the same example of unbelief.

The New Testament book of Hebrews gives us direct insight to our spiritual journey that mirrors the physical journey of the Old Testament Israelites. Hebrews was penned and directed to the descendants of the Israelites, the Hebrew people of the Promised Land journey. The story of the journey to arrive and stay in the land they occupied was well known to them as part of their history and culture. The author of Hebrews draws on the physical journey to the Promised Land as a comparison to our current spiritual destination, the Place of Rest.

Hebrews tells us we have an intended destination determined by God. It is referred to as "that rest" in the Authorized King James Version and as a "Place of Rest" in the Contemporary English Version, God's Word, and The Message Bible. It is clear from the writer that we too are on our own journey to our own Promised Land. There is a target, an actual goal, a safe harbor for our New Testament spiritual journey.

Without a target, we drift aimlessly. But if you have a destination in mind, you can determine how to obtain that objective. There is a target and a path or plan to achieve the goal. Someone once said, "If you aim at nothing, you will always hit it." Thank God we have a mark, an objective, a point to place on our spiritual map so we can focus our efforts. And having that target, we can also know when we have arrived.

Compare God's Three Earthly Havens

God has three earthly places of refuge, or havens, He has set forth and described in scripture: the Garden of Eden, the Promised Land, and the Place of Rest. They have some things in common. They are all places that belong to God. They are His; He owns them.

The Garden of Eden

God owned the Garden of Eden. Man was placed in the Garden to tend it and care for it. You might say Adam was the first COO

(Chief Operating Officer) or CEO (Chief Executive Officer). Adam was not the owner, but the manager. I think if you had arrived and asked for the janitor, he would have answered to that as well. Those high officeholders manage the company, but they don't own it. They are hired or appointed by the owners or stockholders to operate the company to its fullest potential.

The owner of the Garden of Eden was and still is God. When Adam disagreed with the owner on the matter of responsibilities, he was fired and evicted from the premises. God barred the door to the Garden and has not permitted Adam or his subordinates to enter the Garden to this day. If Adam wanted to stay in the Garden, he was going to have to give God His rightful place as owner. When Adam usurped that position, he was relieved of his duties and privileges as manager.

The Promised Land

God owned the Promised Land, giving Him the authority to covenant the property to Abraham as a possession, rewarding him for his faithfulness. It may have been occupied by people of different tribes, but God had the power as owner to give its management position to whomever He chose. Just as Adam was placed in the Garden to tend it, so Abraham and his descendants were promised the gift of the Promised Land to possess as caretakers.

It is very important to note that it was for the Israelites to possess, not to own. We use similar terms when we refer to renters of a house—they have possession of the home and the key, but they are not the owners. The owner, called the landlord, may have to knock at the door and not barge in, but make no mistake, when the conditions of the lease are not met by the renter, the landlord will evict them.

Leviticus 25:23 (CEV)

No land may be permanently bought or sold.
It all belongs to me—it isn't your land,
and you only live there for a little while.

God owns this whole planet and no one can claim any part as an owner. We may possess as caretakers or tenants in common a portion of it, but that does not make us the owner. We can possess and defend parts against other people who would try to take over our possession of it, but owning is another matter. Just like Adam was only a caretaker or manager in the Garden, so the people of the Promised Land were only tenants to manage, not owners.

That does not mean anyone can take the Promised Land from Israel. God, the greatest power of the universe, has sublet it to them and will defend that lease. Israel does not need to defend it, since the owner, God, has made that His priority and has staked His word and reputation on its endurance.

Ownership of the Promised Land can best be understood as we see how many times the descendants of Abraham, Isaac, and Jacob have been in the land and how many times they were removed. The owner has never been removed, but the managers keep getting evicted. The God of second and third chances gives them opportunities to possess the land again on some conditions. When they fail those conditions, the owner, God, evicts them and sends them away, just like He did to Adam in the Garden.

The scriptures do promise possession of the Promised Land will ultimately be Israel, but the owner will always be God. Israel will have the lease, but not the land. God still owns the Promised Land and all the rest of the earth. He will make it desolate, shake it, rock it, or even flood it if He so desires. He can also give the possession of it to whomever He appoints to maintain it.

There are those who read into the scripture that the Promised Land is "given" to Israel, and therefore they own it. But if God, the greatest power of the universe, had given them ownership rather than possession, why did he evict them so many times? We should look at the gift as a right to possess, not to own. God is still God. God still owns everything. David tells us in Psalm 24:1 (CEV), "The earth and everything on it belong to the LORD. The world and its people belong to Him." He gives leases, not ownership. We try to turn our leases into ownership to our own destruction. Our own warped point of view leads us to wrong conclusions.

The Place of Rest

The New Testament Place of Rest is not a physical location, but a spiritual haven we can live in if we have given ownership of our lives to God. That is far more than just a mental acknowledgement—it is a practical mindset that God owns everything about us. It is not that we give ownership over to God. It is more that we stop taking ownership from Him. He is the owner, if we can just stop stepping in front of Him. The Place of Rest is that spiritual place where you can live as a Christian allowing God to retain ownership.

It is a restful place because you don't have to fight your battles; they are God's battles and He will fight them. If I allow Him to keep ownership, that means He also owns every detail about me. He is the owner and responsible for solving all the problems I may have. In this place, we do not take God's responsibility from Him. He retains His care and oversight of us as His property.

It is a peaceful place because the decisions are no longer ours. God will want us to manage our appointed place well, but in the end, the final decisions are God's. When you were the final decision maker (owner), you had to take the fall for every wrong decision and try to get the glory for every correct choice. But with God as the owner, He gets the Glory and He must clean up the mess if He were to make a bad call. But that is where trust comes in. God does not make any bad choices. We may take some time figuring out what He is doing, but God makes no mistakes. Psalm 37:25 tells us, "I have been young, and now am old; yet have I not seen the righteous forsaken, nor his seed begging bread."

Shadrach, Meshach, and Abednego had perfect peace when they told King Nebuchadnezzar they would not bow down to worship his golden idol. They knew God owned them. They trusted God would make the right choice. They had confidence God could correct any situation that might seem to not go in their direction. When the greatest power in the universe is your owner and overseer, you can "bet the farm" on it; it is a certainty. He has it all within His power to solve. Don't step out from under his protective umbrella to go it alone on your own. Trust Him. The magnificent story of their trust in the Almighty who walked with them through the fire as their owner is told in the book of Daniel, chapter three.

Daniel could face the lion in the den because he knew who owned the lion. He knew who his owner was. The lion would have to do what God commanded or get evicted from the cage. Daniel was staying in the cage and wasn't going to take ownership of himself, the lion, or the cage. *Grab a pillow, let's get some sleep,* he must have thought. *God has this in the bag.*

It is calming to know God has your back. Not just your back— He has you in the palm of His hand. Don't take yourself out of

His hand no matter what. Just like the victory in the Promised Land was won forty years previously for the Israelites, so our battle is already won, if we just believe. They could have walked into the Promised Land, watched the foe run, and enjoyed the victory. In like manner, we can rest in knowing the battle is already won, watch how He accomplishes it, and enjoy the victory provided, because we did not take the battle from Him.

The Valley of the Shadow of Death

I gave my wife a kiss goodbye and hugged my children for what could have been the last time. I was at perfect peace as I walked away from them into the prep room for the operation. God had this. I knew He was the owner of the problem and me. Whatever the outcome, I would accept it. I could echo the words of Job 13:15: "Though he slay me, yet will I trust in him." I was in God's hand and always had been.

It had been just five weeks since the MRI had revealed the tumor. There had always been some minor reasons for the symptoms and migraines. Various medical professionals had used allergies, stress, and even eyestrain to explain the evidence that had manifested over time. For all the years I'd had the tumor, there had been no major symptoms and no discernible change until now. In the last several months, I had noticed my vision diminishing in brightness. Initially, I hadn't given it much thought. But then a sudden, dramatic difference in vision quality as I blinked one eye and then the other forced me into seeking medical attention.

When the eye doctor found nothing wrong with my eyes, he sent me for an MRI. It took a month to get the MRI scheduled and completed. The technician who ran the MRI was as friendly as I was. But when he handed me the disk with the electronic scans on it, he told me, "Get this to your doctor as fast as you can." He could not interpret it at his pay grade, but he knew I needed to rush.

The first neurosurgeon I visited showed us the tumor on the scans. Because it had grown past the size that existing ratings scales listed for similar tumors, he could not give a detailed prognosis. It was a bigger and more difficult task than he had ever done. My wife and I stood shocked as he pointed out the tumor and its size on the MRI. It occupied the area from the base of my brain to the last vertebra of the spine. The bone cap covering the pituitary gland had been pushed aside. The tumor sat near the carotid artery and filled the nerve passage from the back of the eyes to the base of the brain. It stretched the optic nerves to the point of breaking and endangered the main artery supplying blood to my brain. He made a phone call to the top neural surgery hospital in the country and inquired how soon their top surgeons could see me. We were at Emory in Atlanta the next week.

Emory is a research hospital and takes on the impossible, even if it is to gain knowledge or stretch the boundaries of medical science. I had the top surgeon in the country. Would you expect any less from the God who owns you and cares for you better than you would for yourself?

The surgeon, who had done several hundred of these operations on smaller tumors, made sure we understood the risks. The list was long but included blindness, paralysis, brain death, and just plain death. The surgeon had to deal with the main artery, the optic nerves, and the membrane protecting the brain. He estimated the surgery might be one of his longer ones, taking all of three hours.

The surgery was authorized and scheduled two weeks out. I had two weeks!

In those two weeks, I had perfect peace. I didn't try to fill a bucket list or travel to somewhere I'd always wanted to go. On the contrary, I knew my God owned this problem. I belonged to Him; therefore, all my problems were His. Why should I worry when the most powerful force in the universe had this covered?

When we told the children what was ahead, it was with the simple words "Just relax, stand back, and watch God perform miracles." I wanted them to have the same confidence I had in Him. It was not a time to worry, but a time to praise Him for what He could and would do.

God gave me the opportunity to go through the fire with Shadrach, Meshach, and Abednego. I was going with the same words: "My God shall deliver me, but if not, I still will not trust any other but HIM." Like Daniel, I knew I would be able to say, "I am well for God shut the mouth of the Lions." If you let God own your greatest problem, you can sleep soundly in the "Place of Rest" with the "peace of God, which passeth all understanding" (Philippians 4:7).

After the operation, I awoke in a hospital room. I could not speak or move, but I knew I was alive. I could feel my wife holding my hand. I could hear voices. I spoke, but no one could understand the noises that came out of me. I tried several times to speak. Finally, the words became clear and they adjusted my pillow as I had been asking them to do. The surgery had lasted eight hours and required two additional emergency deliveries of blood to the hospital. But God had not failed me. I could repeat with the angel who said in Genesis 18:14, "Is any thing too hard for the LORD?"

Whatever your problem, don't touch it; your owner
has it covered.
You can rest in peace in "His Rest."

Psalm 23:4

Yea, though I walk through the valley of the
shadow of death,
I will fear no evil: for thou art with me.

God still had a purpose for me here. I had not yet penned
Forgive Instantly & Live Free, which would go on to help many find
the key to peace with God and themselves. How could I have
guessed what lay ahead, that I would explore His ownership to
great depths and attempt to pass deep truths on to those willing
to give everything back to Him?

CHAPTER 8

LOST IN TRANSLATION

1 Corinthians 13:12 (CEV)

Now all we can see of God is like a cloudy picture
in a mirror.
Later we will see him face to face.
We don't know everything, but then we will,
just as God completely understands us.

The Bible was originally written in three languages: Hebrew, Koine Greek, and Chaldean. The book of Daniel was penned in the ancient language of the Chaldeans, used in Babylon where Daniel was a captive at the height of the Babylonian Empire. Koine Greek of the New Testament time is not a spoken language today. Current-day Greeks cannot read or understand the Koine Greek of two thousand years ago, just as we would find it hard to recognize many of the words of the 1611 King James translation. Our King James Bible is termed the Authorized King James and dates to 1769. English had evolved a great deal in one hundred fifty years from 1611 to 1769.

Languages are in a continual state of change. The printing press slowed the rate of change, but did not stop it. If a Civil War soldier were to show up by way of time machine into our present world, how would you explain a computer, a telephone, or even an automobile without showing him one? Because the world and people change, language must also change to keep up.

Koine Greek was a rich language that had far more words than English. Koine Greek had seven words for love, whereas English had one. Since no one spoke or used Koine Greek in 1611, to determine the meaning of the words, a person had to compare the Greek text to later Latin translations and writings and the early church commentators and historians of the day—who wrote about the New Testament in various languages—to find context for the original words.

We will not go too deep into the topic, nor will we try to solve the mystery surrounding the differences between the two basic sources of ancient Greek texts. These sources are the texts originating out of Antioch in Asia Minor and those from Alexandria, Egypt. They differ slightly in the number of verses they contain and some phrases missing in the Alexandria texts.

The Bible scholars reading this will be disturbed at me for not taking a side on the argument of which is correct, since both have a lot of passion for their position and good reasons for their view. Still, the differences in the texts are small and affect no doctrine. Because none of us were alive when the texts were written, we cannot produce eyewitnesses who can declare with certainty that we absolutely know which is correct. We have our opinions based on what we see in the evidence we have. We will leave this debate for God to solve and protect His holy scriptures.

The Craft of Translating

Translation is more of an art than a science. It is subject to opinions, usage, and the background of the translator. Because translators do not work in a vacuum, but already have a belief system and a certain view of God and the world, they tend to choose words that reflect their mindset. They also have the culture they live in, the country where they were raised, and the particular education and educators who influenced them. In other words, they are human, and not inspired. Since only the original text can claim inspiration, we struggle to do our best to produce a version in English that we can get the most out of. For that reason, we strive to keep up with our shifts in language and word usage to make the Bible as meaningful to readers as possible. There are over fifty versions of the Bible in English to date. The Authorized King James (KJV) is used by over 50 percent of readers in the United States. The New International Version takes second place with 19 percent. The Voice (VOICE), Holman Christian Standard (HCSB), Good News Bible (GNB), Contemporary English Version (CEV), and Bible in Basic English (BBE) are gaining popularity with readers.

The 1611 King James Times and Culture

England in the early 1600s had a certain unique culture and language that influenced the translation of the King James Bible. Because of the feudal system in place at the time, two different

Greek words were translated, with one English word using capitals as the only contrast between the two. The word "lord" appears in the King James Bible approximately seven hundred times, occasionally capitalized as "LORD."

LORD

The Hebrew word "YHWH" is often brought in to English as "Yahweh" to make it pronounceable. It is the proper, most-high name for God and is translated in the King James as "LORD" with all capital letters in both the Old and New Testaments.

The name is made up of four Hebrew consonants coming from the first letter of different words. It is called the Tetragrammaton. YHWH used in the Hebrew Bible as the unspoken name for God is the first letter of the Hebrew words for "always existed," "exists now," and "always will exist." If we were to translate that name, we would use "The Eternal One," or "Ever-Existent One." Some of the new translations use these names for God. It is a refreshing change and brings clarity to the reader. The eternal aspect of the name makes it impossible for that name to apply to any other person or entity other than God. It can only refer to God.

Lord

"Kyrios" is a New Testament Greek word that means "owner," as in the supreme creator and rightful owner who is the inventor and manufacturer. In feudal England, the owner of land was the lord of the realm. So to seventeenth-century England, "lord" was the best word to use for the Greek word to signify God's high position as owner of the universe. It was a correct translation for them at the time. It was a descriptive word and not a proper name.

By comparison, Lord Cromwell would have been a description, the owner, coupled with a proper name.

Kyrios is a description of God's position and is translated "Lord" with only the first letter capitalized. "LORD" refers to the proper name of God, while the other, "Lord (Kyrios)," describes God's position as supreme owner.

Language Evolves and Is Ever Changing

Over time, the King James Version has transformed the words in our minds to a generic term for God. We read through the King James text without making any distinction and let the words morph into a common reference with less impact than "Our Father." It neither carries the weight of His proper name nor the power of His position as supreme owner. It has become a simple reference to God or Jesus depending on the context.

An unfortunate problem was created with one word being used in English for two different concepts. One usage was a proper name, the other a description of position. Over time, and far from the scholars who set the difference in capital contrasted with small letters, we meld the words into a single reference for God.

Time and People March On

Over the decades, our culture has changed. In 1773, we Americans threw the British tea in the Boston Harbor. We declared independence in 1776. We got rid of dukes and earls. We shed the titles of princes and princesses, kings and queens. We dropped any references to counts and barons. We also did away with lords. "Lord" was the term for royalty and was a title given to those who were owners of land estates.

Americans were eye to eye with each other, equal in birth and without title. Land was so abundant; nearly all could own a place to build a home. Just venture out a little farther in the woods and find a spot to call home. In shedding all those titles from our language, we no longer called a landowner "lord" since the majority could own land. We still have one word left in our language as a vestige of those times: "landlord."

As we look at the English language in the time of the translation of the King James Bible, we can easily see that the word "Lord" used in the Bible fit a particular attribute of God. He was the owner. So the Greek word "Kyrios" was translated some six hundred times, with the word "Lord" meaning the supreme owner. It was correct for their time. But times have changed.

Several times, Kyrios is translated "master." We used the term early in our country's history to refer to a schoolmaster. It is still used in Great Britain to designate the head of an independent school. The schoolmasters held positions of utmost authority at the top of the school system.

Over the course of four hundred years, this unfortunate use of the same word created a loss in meaning and understanding. We diminished God's proper name to a common term. But far worse, we have lost sight of God as our owner. Just as Adam diminished God's position as owner of the Garden, so we have followed in Adam's path by diminishing—in our minds—God's position as our owner.

We have lost the concept of HIS OWNERSHIP in our relationship with HIM and in our daily life. It fits into our nature we inherited from Adam to be the owner of our own destiny, our own universe, and have God at our fingertips as though we own

Him—quite simply, to be our own God. We have a natural tendency to let our language and terms expose how we see ourselves and the world. We view the world and God through the distorted, flawed lenses we inherited from Adam. Given the opportunity, man will shrink God's position as owner and will elevate himself to that role. Our imagination has no limit to our being God. We like being God. We think the opposite of John the Baptist when he said, "He must increase, but I must decrease," in John 3:30.

Fortunately, the tide may be turning. The new Voice version translates "Kyrios" some three hundred times using the word "owner." It is refreshing to see the deeper meanings coming into use. Some have argued that the new translations weaken the scriptures. I would contend they strengthen the meaning and bring the Bible into focus so we can follow its teachings more easily.

Bias in Translation

Matthew 16:24

If any man will come after me, let him deny himself,
and take up his cross, and follow me.

The spiritual level and understanding of the translator is a critical factor in the final results of a translation. The rendering will go no higher than the level the linguists have achieved in their own personal relationship with God. They will not convey a principle they cannot see or possibly don't understand.

The request Jesus makes in Matthew 16:24 is an example of bias creeping into the text. The Greek word "aparneomai," translated in the King James as "deny," actually means to "disown." Every word has a list of possible synonyms and a description of its usage. As the translators ponder a word, their view of Christianity influences the choices they make in rendering a meaning. In this case, they picked a word much less empathic concerning the commitment needed to follow. Because disowning is extreme and very hard to accomplish, the translators may have not understood or been living the principle to have noticed the error. We can blame our human condition not wanting to see the maxim of His ownership that crept into their rendering. All of us would have missed the impact of this word sometime in our life.

There is a mile of difference between "deny" and "disown." To deny is relatively easy to do since it is open to levels of thought and meaning. We practice it every Lenten season as we deny something in order to show our identity with the Savior's gift of His life. What a weak comparison to think denying chocolate for forty days would somehow reflect the immense price Jesus paid on the cross for us!

The word "disown" is a total commitment that cannot be contained in forty days. It is a sovereign concept that is total and final in its pledge. To disown is to give up all control and claim. It is hard for us to make that large leap into God's hand. The more education we have, the more we glory in our ability, the harder it is to give the ownership of "our" glory to the one who made us who and what we are. (It is the creator's glory, not ours.)

Young's Literal Translation was among the earliest and few to render the word correctly. We expect accuracy from a translation that puts the word "literal" in its title. The YLT shows intense directive must be mandated to overcoming bias against God's ownership. A descendant of Adam will likely choose a word that favors humanity and slights God if given the option.

King James Only

I recognize that there is a large group of King James–only followers who will not be too happy with the use of other versions. I too hold a reverence for the King James Bible. Its poetic style always makes a person sit up a little straighter when they hear the "thee" and "thou" of the old English rather than "you" and "your." There is a clear distinction that lets you know you are reading sacred text. I get that and I love it just like many of you. I will always use the King James as a basic starting point. It is from the King James Version that I memorized so much scripture with its dignified style.

But we must recognize we have not done as well with following its precepts as much as we have in disagreeing with one another about its words. Jesus said in John 13:35, "By this shall all men know that ye are my disciples, if ye have love one to another." He did not say, "By this shall all men know that you are my disciples, if you hold fast to the ancient language." If that were the case, we would still be speaking Koine Greek, not sixteenth-century English. Let's try to concentrate on following what Jesus gave us. The best way to do that is to understand His concepts in the clearest language we have. Let's get His meaning as He intended, and then let's do the things He asks. Let's follow Him.

I am not asking you to follow me. I am pointing to Jesus, trying to clarify what He said and meant, and asking you to follow HIM.

CHAPTER 9

THE DISCOVERY

Psalm 11:3

If the foundations be destroyed,

what can the righteous do?

I stumbled on what I view as the greatest truth in the Bible by accident. It is the foundational truth that all the scriptures rest on. I did not hear or learn about it in the churches I attended or in seminary. It is a truth hidden from most Christians. It is clearly stated in the scriptures, but rarely explored or put in practice. In fact, we are so blind to this truth, we find it hard to see that we are missing it in our daily lives. Even now, when I tell you what the truth is, you might think it's a waste of time or that it is too simple to be important. Look carefully. This one truth alone will change your thinking, your life, and your entire view of the scriptures.

It is the foundation that many haven't noticed. We often look at houses, but seldom see the foundation they rest on. But without the foundation, the building would fall.

The truth I found is God's ***ownership*** status. It is not just a truth to acknowledge, but a truth to live by. We may acknowledge mentally that God owns everything, but we do not practice it in our daily lives. We only ask God for advice or help in a crisis because we still own the problem and ourselves. His help is greatly appreciated in the handling of "our" problems. But in small matters, we may not ask at all. We view God as either a candy store or a manager to hire, but never consider Him to be the owner of the problem or ourselves. As the owner, He would be responsible for solving the whole thing.

The real truth is that God owns you and therefore owns the problems you have. It is not your problem that you should ask His help to solve. If you acknowledge Him as your owner and the problem's owner, you simply ask Him if He would like your help with solving the problem, or if He would prefer you to stand back and wait for Him to solve it on His own. God's ownership offers a whole new way to look at your life and the world you live in. Getting this right will change your life forever.

The Path to the Abundant Life

In Matthew 7:14, Matthew writes, "[T]he gate is small and the road is narrow that leads to true life. Only a few people find that road" (NCV). He is obviously not talking about salvation through faith in Christ since over two billion people claim to believe in Christ, which is not a few. He is referring to the Abundant Life, the true life, the life He has set aside for you to enjoy. It is described as the "Place of Rest" and the "peace of God" that passes all understanding. He is talking about the victorious Christian life. You may think you have it. You may, or you may not. Many think they are at the top of their game in their Christian walk. They view it through their own lens, but God's view may be different. We want to know the difference between the regular Christian life and the abundant Christian life. We want to see what this life is from His view and then make the judgment as to whether we have His best.

The predisposition to own is hard to identify and confess, because we live in its grasp and under its spell. We have the sin of being God so deeply embedded in our soul and spirit, we find it difficult to understand God's point of view. We are saturated with "owning" as if we were marinated in it.

My Journey of Discovery

My journey started in the valley, the dark places of failure and disappointment. I did not know the cause, but I had anger issues associated with being a perfectionist. Perfectionists are always frustrated and angry because nothing is ever perfect. It also makes a person critical of others and often is the source of relationship difficulties and failures. To some degree, we may all have some tendencies toward perfectionism. In the Old Testament, Isaiah 53:6 (NLV) tells us, "All of us like sheep have gone the wrong way. Each of us has turned to his own way." We want things our own way. Notice the word "own." Yes, we own our way. It is mine, the way I want it. We all have that problem to some degree, according to Isaiah, who under God's inspiration said we do. Yes, he said *all*. We all share this inherited flaw of insisting on our own way, because we are Adam's offspring; he started us down that path.

For years, I had tried to manage and control my anger. Just when I thought I was doing well, some incident would surprise me; the reaction was equally swift and surprising. I dated a girl who blew up over some little incident that seemed small to me or even unnoticeable by most people. Why such a negative reaction to such a small event? Later I learned we both suffered from the same problem—we had a lot of baggage from childhood hurts.

In digging deep for a spiritual solution for my anger, I discovered Mark 7:15. It reads, "There is nothing from without a man, that entering into him can defile him: but the things which come out of him, those are they that defile the man." In the Amplified Bible, it reads, "There is nothing outside a man which by going into him can defile him; but the things which come out of the heart of a man are what defile *and* dishonor him."

I could not get my mind off that truth. For days, I pondered that verse. I read it in every translation I could get my hands on. I did not want to accept it. Clearly, *I* was the one harming and causing havoc in my life. I had been blaming others for so long. In my way of thinking, it was always someone else who was less than perfect creating my problem. The Gospel writer was telling me that I was the problem—there was something inside me that needed correcting. To find a cure, I had to discover what was inside me. If you don't know what you're hunting for, you can't expect to find it.

Having always concentrated on the Gospels, I searched and read Jesus's words once again. The Lord's Prayer caught my attention. Matthew 6:12 had been translated in several different ways. The

KJV reads, "And forgive us our debts, as we forgive our debtors." Some used the word "trespasses" while others used "offenses." Clearly, they were trying to take the thought of a monetary debt out of the translation, but what was correct?

I opened the Greek lexicon to see for myself. "Debt" was the correct choice. The Lord's Prayer had such a spiritual tone—why did one phrase jump to the temporal subject of money and debt? It was my narrow-mindedness that created the roadblock. After connecting "offense" and "trespasses" with "debt," I saw they were all the same thing. It was not a financial debt, but a spiritual debt. When someone offended me, I created a debt against them for an apology or some other restitution they owed me to right their wrongs.

I had discovered the psychological meaning of the word baggage. Sometime in our lives, we start holding on to a debt that someone owes us for their wrongdoing. Those debts accumulate if we don't find a way to forgive and release them. Our preference is to collect on them and get the apology we deserve. Some of the debts are huge, with entire childhoods being owed. Some carry the debts created by the loss of dignity or respect. Others hold grudges against those who abused them or harmed them, always waiting for the chance to collect or even pay back the harm and wishing ill on the offender. In all cases, these are kept in the heart as baggage or debts. Hebrews calls this the "bitterness" of life (Hebrews 12:15).

My baggage was hidden from me. Thanks to God's genius design of the human mind, I had been able to hide the hurts I had suffered deep in the recesses of my heart so I could live and function without haunting memories disrupting my day. But the effects of the debt kept coming out, even though I had the memories and experiences all wrapped in a nice package that could not be easily seen. It took failure, pain, and agony in my everyday life to scrape off the layers of camouflage to discover the debts hidden in my mind.

We can bury unpleasant life events and the tremendous hurts we have suffered by surrounding them with a mental block that clouds our memory of them. Our body does the same thing when it forms a cyst. It creates a barrier around a harmful substance to protect us from it. The first time I was bitten by a no-see-um near the rim of my hat, the venom was so toxic to my system that my body formed a cyst around it to isolate it. Years later, I had it surgically removed because when I wore a hat in the sunny New Mexico mountains, it irritated the cyst. Just as my body had tried to protect me from the bite, our mind will bury our hurt in a hidden closet of the heart to protect us from the pain. To be healthy and whole again, we must have the heartaches and baggage removed.

In my relationships, when I received constructive criticism, I learned to listen and heed the advice. In earlier times, I had viewed constructive comments as pure criticism from poor sources. When I viewed their words as helpful, I discovered problems within that led me to my baggage, the people and events that had wounded me.

The scriptures give us God's method for solving bitterness from the past. The Sermon on the Mount, recorded of Jesus in the Gospel of Matthew, transcends our normal lives and gives us the road map to the highest level of living that Jesus designed for us. In the Beatitudes, He gives the steps to achieving that Abundant Life. In these steps, I found the key to clearing the heart of debt.

The key was in Matthew 5:8. It reads, "Blessed are the pure in heart: for they shall see God." The word "pure" is translated from the Greek word "katharos." We have words in English that come from that Greek origin. "Katharos" means "to drain." Cathode tubes in our old television sets were used to drain the electrical charge off the screen so the next set of electrons could display a new image and create movement. Without the rapid draining of the charge from the last picture, only a blur would be visible. We also have catheters to drain body fluids after operations or sickness.

In this message, Jesus conveys that we cannot be happy until we've drained past baggage from our hearts. The only way to empty the heart of its past bitter disappointments is to forgive. If you wait to get an apology or payment for the debt, you may die before it comes. What a waste of the Christian life to have carried things that are destroying you when you could have drained them from your heart by forgiving! That is why Jesus called offenses "debts."

Forgiving is not just issuing a pardon to let the offender off the hook, but it is the canceling of the debt we hold inside. To give a pardon without draining the debt does not free a person from the problem. It is so important to verbally issue a cancellation by saying, "You don't owe me anymore. I am not going to try to collect from you ever again." That drains the debt and sets you free.

At the end of the verse, the word "see" comes from the translation of a Greek word that means to deeply inspect, different from a casual look. Once you've drained your heart, you can more easily see God. We might say, "Oh, I see" when we want to let someone know we understand. In this message, He is literally saying, "Those who drain their heart will have a deeper understanding of God."

It is not my intent to teach forgiveness as outlined in my first book, *Forgive Instantly & Live Free*. That book details how to set yourself free using the power of forgiveness. I only want to give you the background in this chapter so you understand what led to the greatest discovery of all.

I dumped all my baggage in one shot. For an hour, in my mind, I paraded offenders in front of me and cancelled the debts I held against them. This was my debt. I did not need them present to cancel that debt. It was not about reconciliation or relationship recovery—this was saving my own heart from self-destruction. Forgiving requires only one person—you. Once I forgave, I was free of my past. The anger was gone.

The Lightbulb Moment

Soon after, I found myself simmering over a new offender and a new offense. All my deep, embedded anger was gone, so my reactions were now calm and collected, but I had to consider the event and the person who had just offended me. I had developed four words to live by: "Forgive everyone for everything." Now I was faced with having to forgive in real time. Some offenses took days, but always I had to forgive. Each event left unattended or unforgiven could destroy what peace and harmony I had gained by forgiving.

I had to find a way to forgive rapidly to not sink back into old ways. Jesus had forgiven his killers in the middle of their deed, without their asking for forgiveness. That was fast, immediate. I added the word "instantly" to the four words and searched for a way to accomplish it. That was beyond my ability. I needed help. The search drove me back to the Sermon on the Mount for answers.

The last phrase of the Lord's Prayer contains the secret: "For thine is the kingdom, and the power, and the glory, for ever" (Matthew 6:13b). The "for" stands out. It is a foundation word. The Lord's Prayer to this point focuses on the grand truths and requests as if they are a house or building, but now it speaks of the foundation the structure was built on. All the requests and precepts of the prayer would be done because "THINE is the kingdom, the power, and the glory forever." "Thine" is an ownership word. Because everything belongs to God, the items in the prayer could be accomplished. The entire prayer is built on the foundation that God owns the kingdom, the power, and the glory.

I considered what it means to own something. An owner is responsible for what he owns. If an item is damaged, he is on the hook for the repair. If you damage a car, you pay the owner for the damage. You do not pay the car! If you let God take ownership, instant forgiveness is easy. If someone offends you, they owe God and not you. If you have given God ownership, they pay God the apology—after all, they damaged His property. Since the offense was not against you, you can forgive instantly. If you let Him own your problems, you can stop worrying about them, because they are not yours. I don't remember witnessing an accident and worrying about the damage inflicted on other people's cars.

I saw the whole world differently. Scripture began to make sense. I had been lost in the forest of verses, but now I could step back and see the bigger picture from beginning to end. This whole mess is about man stealing the ownership away from God as Adam did in the Garden, and we have continued to commit that crime, that offense against God, every day since. I embarked on a new journey to discover the whole of God's ownership of this world and its people.

CHAPTER 10

TWO LEVELS OF CHRISTIAN LIFE

Ephesians 2:8–9 (GW)

God saved you through faith as an act of kindness.

You had nothing to do with it.

Being saved is a gift from God.

It's not the result of anything you've done,

so no one can brag about it.

No Skyscrapers

I see Christianity as a two-story building. It is neither a twelve-story building nor a forty- or even a hundred-story skyscraper. Jesus and other writers of the New Testament refer to just two different layers of Christian living.

Some view our faith as a multilevel system where you enter at the ground level as a new convert and learn and grow in knowledge and behavior, gaining higher levels of stature as you mature in Christ. They have levels for those in full-time Christian work, and levels for Sunday school teachers, soul winners, and prayer warriors.

This type of thinking is not found in Scripture. In fact, the very opposite is quoted in Matthew 19:30, Mark 10:31, and Luke 13:30, all referring to Jesus's words: "The last shall be first and the first shall be last." Mankind will always seek ways to elevate his stature in the eyes of others. Our very nature of wanting to own everything causes us to promote ourselves, our reputation and prestige. We strive to gain a superior position to others. We manufacture levels, honors, awards, degrees, and titles to highlight our self-important status.

I am always dismayed when I see a church billboard advertising location and service times when the lettering on the pastor's name is large and predominant. It is even more discouraging when titles and degrees of the speaker are listed with boldness. Are we trying to get followers for the church leaders or are we trying to get people to follow Jesus? Our pride of life leads us into a multitier pattern of thinking. The more titles we give ourselves, the farther from Him we are. We have nothing to glory in or take credit for; all we are and have has been provided by Him.

Isaiah 64:8 (ESV)

But now, O LORD, you are our Father;
we are the clay, and you are our potter;
we are all the work of your hand.

I am overwhelmed by a simple verse given to us by the apostle John when he quoted some seekers who had come to find Jesus, but were unable to access Him because the disciples were in the way, as if they were gatekeepers of the Savior. John 12:21 quotes them saying, "Sir, we would see Jesus." If we are pointing more at ourselves instead of the Savior, we can get in the way of seekers from finding Jesus. We are inclined to stand in for God and speak for Him. We steal His power and glory when we take the stage with a know-it-all attitude.

Two-Story Building

God always makes things much simpler than our way of thinking. Jesus said, "I have come to give them life and life more abundantly" (John 10:10). He speaks about the possibility of having life and adds a second choice, the possibility of having Abundant Life. So, Jesus only gives us two levels of living out our time here in this earthly journey. When the disciples, with their multilevel thinking, asked Jesus who would be greater, He pulled the rug out from under them with His comment "The first shall be last" (Mark 9:34–35).

The ground-floor level of our faith is where most Christians live. You get into the building by believing in Jesus. That is your entrance to a grand adventure in following Him. On this first level are many different jobs to do. We need some to serve as pastors and teachers. We need missionaries willing to go outside to win others and bring them into the building. We need song leaders and servants to wait tables. On this wilderness level, we also struggle to shed the things we brought with us from the outside. But no matter what our job is while we are here on this ground level, we are all equal. Some will get paid for their work, some will work as volunteers, but all are in the ministry of helping each other. All are on their own journey at their own speed to hunt for and find the happiness Jesus foretold is in the next level, the Abundant Life, the second story of the building.

Our First-Story Adventure—Getting in the Door

Getting folks into the first floor of Christianity is something God has called us to do by carrying the message of salvation to those who do not know or follow Him. But once in the door, they are to follow Jesus, not people. They can learn from us by watching us, but they are to follow Him. We can teach scripture and help them to learn, but it is God who changes hearts and minds.

Ephesians 2:8–9 tells us there is only one way to heaven—by grace. All other man-made ways are dead ends and characterized as "works." The King James Version reads, "For by grace are ye saved through faith; and that not of yourselves: it is the gift of God. Not of works, lest any man should boast." He puts all the religions of the world into one category called "works." If you are not coming to Him by grace, which is God's way, you are in some system created by man, which will involve some means of work to earn your way. All of man's systems fail because they are not God's way. People invent religions that promote man and his ability. God's plan is simple and straightforward. He provided safe passage to heaven and a pardon to get you through any judgment by providing a gift of Jesus's sacrifice.

John 3:16 promises, "[W]hosoever believeth in Him should not perish, but have everlasting life." It is a great adventure and a growing process as we learn and adjust to His way of living. None of us are giants in the faith on day one. We all have a lot to learn. We have a lot of transformation and changing in our behavior, mind, and attitudes as we search to find the Abundant Life He alludes to.

It is more important to change mindset than behavior. If you change behavior without an attitude adjustment, the old habits will return. But if you change the mindset, it will in turn affect your behavior. Because the mindset changed, the behavior changes will be permanent. The underlying character of the mind governs the external behavior.

There are critics who throw out the term "easy believe-ism." They claim that to be a Christian, you must show repentance and great change of life. They scoff at bringing people to Jesus without drilling them in a regimented course of doctrine and behavior. They are referred to in 1 Samuel 16:7 as those who "looketh on the outward appearance, but the LORD looketh on the heart." It is scripture that tells us to concentrate on the heart. God will do the convicting of sin and foster the miracles it takes to change a person inside and out. We are to center our teachings on changing attitudes of the mind and heart, for "out of [the heart] are the issues of life" (Proverbs 4:23). By stressing outward behavior, we only appear judgmental to the outside world.

Living on the First Floor—Normal Christian Life as Owners

In the ground floor or main level that most of us spend a large portion of our lives on is where we maintain a good deal of ownership of our own life and affairs. Outside in the lost world, we were the sole owner of our destiny and details of life. But now, inside on the ground level, we have a new nature, a new direction, a new destiny. Still, it is a hard task to beat that inner, inherited flaw of owning everything in sight, including ourselves.

The sin of being God has been ingrained in us. It is hard for us to see the ownership issue we carry inside. We do not see the real root of sin because it is so much a part of our nature—we are blind to its presence. It is easier to see and work on those things that emanate out of us than to find the core problem that resides inside us. So, we focus on the fruit of the spirit: love, joy, peace, kindness, self-control, and so on, but fail to dig deep for the root that causes all these crop failures.

We have a new influence in our life—God in the form of the Holy Spirit is working in us and through us to refine us. Now we consider, "What would Jesus do?" We have a new direction. As we grow in our newfound faith, we invite more influence and supervision from God. Followers realize that God's influence is good and profitable for a good life.

They will grow to let God manage their life and do their best to have God's plans and desires override their own. They gain a willingness to let God be the manager of their life. They still own their life, but yield to His directives. It is like a corporation hiring a manager. The manager or CEO runs the show if He is doing it successfully or to the owner's approval. But when things go wrong, the manager can be moved aside, sent on vacation, or outright fired. Christians on the first level still live and function as if they own themselves and use God as a helper or manager.

Getting to the Second Story

In our illustration of Christianity being a two-story building, both levels are called "life." One is just more abundant and richer than the other. In attainting the second level, we function with God as our owner. It is not something we grow into. It is something we find. You don't grow so tall that you arrive at the second level. You get to the second level as soon as you find the stairs or elevator that takes you there. We find the key to the Abundant Life, that second level, when we realize God is the owner. The second level has a new relationship with God that is like the original creation that Adam experienced in the Garden before the Fall. Everything functions as though God were the owner.

What is the difference between the first and second level? Who is the owner? The difference is letting God take over as owner, not just manager of your life. Owners can fire managers. Managers do not have the power to fire owners. Therein lies the truth of Matthew 6:13: "Thine is the POWER." He has the power on level two; he can fire you, you can't fire Him.

On the second level, the Abundant Life, God doesn't manage your life, He owns it. As the owner, He can and will put you in a fiery furnace or make you sleep in a lion's den. He can have you swallowed by a great whale, only to spit you out on dry ground so you can go and do the job as He asked. When your owner is as powerful as *my* God, get ready for an exciting life!

Second Level—Owned by God

It was about four in the afternoon. We had been passing out tracts and invitations for several hours to people along the markets in a remote Peruvian village high in the Andes. We had a service scheduled for that evening. Without warning, one of our new disciples grabbed my jacket and pulled me backward into the market enclosure. He jerked me so hard and so fast, I struggled to keep my balance. I looked around to see who and what was happening. He explained he had just saved my life. Knowing Quechua, the Inca Indian language, he heard a group of men nearby who had decided to kill me with a knife. They were deciding which one would do the dastardly deed when my new friend in Christ acted to protect me.

It is a dangerous job to take the Gospel into the enemy's backyard. I am sure those thoughts crossed Jonah's mind when God sent him to Nineveh. He went to declare God's imminent destruction of the city if they did not repent and turn from their wicked ways. God owned Jonah and could send him into a dangerous place to give a message that could get him killed. Coming to a city in desperate times with a message that runs counter to their way of life is a risky adventure.

For a moment, Jonah took ownership. He made his own decision and said no to God, he declared he was on vacation, so he headed in the opposite direction. We humans are so silly. Even when we think we own the situation, we really don't. We just go back to fantasyland on level one. Jonah thought he could return to level one and hide from God. But God still owns level one, even if we don't comprehend it. Jonah was going to Nineveh, like it or not. Traveling to Nineveh in a fine coach or camel caravan is painless, far better than traveling by whale innards. But it is your choice. God owns you. You are going where He sends.

Staying on the second level is not a guarantee. It requires a daily battle against the flesh that wants to have its own way. There were times King David lived on the second level and times he lived on the first. He had times when he acknowledged God as owner as in the Psalm 100:3, where he declares he is but a sheep belonging to God in the pasture that is also owned by God. And there were times when David gave in to that inherited disease of false ownership claims.

CHAPTER 11

IN THE BEGINNING— THE GARDEN OF EDEN

Genesis 2:7–8 (BBE)

And the Lord God made man from the dust of the earth,
breathing into him the breath of life:
and man became a living soul.
And the Lord God made a garden in the east, in Eden;
and there he put the man whom he had made.

The mess we find ourselves in all started in the Garden of Eden. The narrative about the Garden is one of the most misunderstood events that continues to baffle human understanding. The misconception stems from our point of view. We don't see it correctly because we are products of the error that was introduced during the Garden experience. We inherited the flaw and are blind to our own deficit.

The Garden scenario has been viewed as an act of disobedience. God made a rule. Man disobeyed it. From that point of view, a relationship with God is based on behavior. This conclusion leads many misguided souls to think that all they must do to get into heaven is behave a certain way; hence the balanced scales of good works outweighing the bad. That basis is the bottom line of all the man-made religions of the world.

Some Christian denominations have a mixture of faith and works. They emphasize salvation by faith in the Savior, but then place the new follower of Jesus into a system of behavior changes to conform to that group's code of conduct. Again, they are placed on a treadmill of behavior-based religion with the ticket of grace to enter the field.

There are many who try to correct that error, and rightly so. They address the identity we have in Christ apart from our failures or behavior. They point out God's view of us, rather than our own perception or performance. Grace is emphasized over behavior and good intentions. They try to bring the believer to a new perspective of the Christian life. But they often focus on the battle between the two opposing sides. They are often caught trying not to be in the behavior mode. We need to move beyond the battle and address the underlying attitude that creates this whole behavior-oriented dilemma. We are so engrained in our way of thinking that behavior-based religion is all we see and experience.

The Garden incident resulted from an attitude change before the actual act of disobedience. It was not that Adam disobeyed God and ate the fruit he had been told not to, but the attitude that convinced him he could do what he wanted. His failure occurred before he ate the fruit. His attitude failed before his behavior.

God only had one rule. How amazing to think that just one rule could not be followed. Even more astounding is that God thought He only needed one rule. But if the heart or attitudes go amok, even one rule is too much. The rule existed to prove that God was the rule-maker and owner of the Garden. The Garden belonged to God. Adam was a guest in God's Garden—a created, honored guest, but nevertheless, not the owner.

When Adam changed the rule, he became the rule-maker, hence the highest position in charge. He became de facto owner of the Garden, or at least attempted to. That change in the attitude was the root of the action that followed. Because he first thought he was in control, rule-maker, and therefore owner of the Garden, he ate the fruit.

Adam's first mistake was thinking that he was above God in the Garden hierarchy. Adam's second mistake was living out that attitude by doing what he wanted, though it contradicted the real owner's wishes.

His third mistake was hiding. God called for him, but he hid in the Garden thinking God would not find him. He covered his mistake rather than confessing and forsaking it. His fourth mistake was blaming Eve when God gave him a chance to explain. He even blamed God for creating Eve as though God were responsible for her flaw. Proverbs 28:13 reads, "He that covereth his sins shall not prosper: but whoso confesseth and forsaketh them shall have mercy." The truth in that verse is everlasting. It was true at that moment in the Garden when Adam failed time and time again, just as it is true today.

Adam's failure encompassed both extremes; he wanted to own good—the Garden—and give away the bad—responsibility for his failures. He went over the line by blaming Eve, but blaming God for having made her was a fatal miscalculation. It was not a good idea to insult Eve, and even worse to criticize God. That may have been the basis for the first marital-counseling request, but it was certainly the first sign of man's contentious attitude toward his creator. Adam made a serious mistake calling God's character into question.

That ownership issue is the root of man's sin against God and still separates us from God to this day. Even in the Christian world, God's ownership of us is an elusive truth because the Garden event is seen as a behavioral problem, not a property-control issue.

I have raised children and faced behavior problems. All parents do. It is part of the growing-up process. But a misdemeanor problem is not something you lock the children out of the house for. They are issues to correct and learn from. They are misdemeanors with low-level fines or punishments.

The Garden sin resulted in an expulsion from the Garden. That is not a misdemeanor punishment. The expulsion is the kind of punishment reflective of a felony. Along with the eviction from the Garden was the death sentence: "thou shalt surely die" (Genesis 2:17). The punishments rendered tell us that what went wrong with Adam was not minor, but a major problem. This was a felony listed in the law books as "Grand Theft Garden." Adam was attempting to steal the entire Garden and become the rule-maker. He was taking over as owner. His attempt was unsuccessful; he only succeeded in getting himself evicted. God never gave up ownership of the Garden or this earth, and never will.

How could we own the earth? We do not have the wherewithal to keep it spinning. We can be a good tenant and Garden keeper, but not adequate owners.

Job 38:33–38 (CEV)

Do you know the laws that govern the heavens,

and can you make them rule the earth?

Can you order the clouds to send a downpour,

or will lightning flash at your command?

Did you teach birds to know that rain or floods are

on their way?

Can you count the clouds or pour out their water

on the dry, lumpy soil?

We have inherited Adam's sin and carry it in our genes; it flows in our blood. We are born with an ownership mindset. Even babies display symptoms of owning and having things their way. Babies are demanding. They are all born expecting to be provided for. Just be late on a feeding and see the demands put on you to do your job in a timelier manner.

That demanding, ownership mentality is not present in the animal kingdom. As a farm boy, I birthed many animals and have been at bedside (barnside) to watch the early days of animal life. When they are hungry, even from the first hour, they search for and find the dinner plates. There is no yelling or demanding for others to do it for them. No matter how helpless a newborn animal is or what species they come from, they are not born entitled. They make no claim of ownership of life or the planet.

What is the first word babies learn that you don't teach them? It is an ownership word. We get them to say Daddy and Mommy because we prime them. They pick up the meaning of the word *no* because we teach it to them, even though they don't repeat it or say it. But do you recall the first time they used the word "mine"? They learned that without you teaching them. It is the first word they learn on their own. Immediately, you try to unlearn it by telling them to share. Where did they get that word? It is an attitude they inherited and finally found a sound to express it. That mindset is born in us. Thank you, Adam.

CHAPTER 12

THE GARDEN CRIME SCENE INVESTIGATION

Isaiah 14:12–14

How art thou fallen from heaven, O Lucifer, son of
the morning!

how art thou cut down to the ground, which didst
weaken the nations!

For thou hast said in thine heart, I will ascend into heaven,

I will exalt my throne above the stars of God:

I will sit also upon the mount of the congregation,
in the sides of the north:

I will ascend above the heights of the clouds; I will
be like the most High.

The Garden of Eden crime scene is an open and ongoing investigation. The case has never been closed and has not been solved

by the upper management of the Bureau of Human Investigation. The evidence at the scene was contaminated with the presence of a serpent. The witnesses gave conflicting narratives as to whom they thought created the conspiracy and pleaded not guilty to the crime.

Most investigators dismiss the case as unworthy of further research because they conclude it is a simple misdemeanor called "theft by taking" with the value of the merchandise (apples are ten cents each) under the twenty-five-dollar threshold needed to qualify as a felony. The punishment for the incident should have been light. Judges feel the defendants herein known as "tenants of the Garden" were punished enough with the eviction and loss of home and tenancy. They conclude no further punishment is warranted if sufficient behavior modifications are made on the part of the tenants and restitution is rendered.

By contrast, the minority report cites a different motive for the tenants and the serpent and classifies all parties as felons. This report draws on the testimony from the owner's statements given to third-party witnesses. They claim to have evidence of an ongoing conspiracy of a theft ring and information leading to a cache of stolen goods.

The differences between the two reports represent the opposing views of what the true motive was. If the motive was to gain wisdom by knowing the difference between good and evil, then you see the simple act of disobedience was performed with the desire to better oneself. But, if the motive was to be God, or become equal to Him, then the act is a felony known as "Grand Theft Garden," punishable by death.

When we see God's reaction, we must conclude that in His view, this was no mere act of disobedience punishable with a time-out, but rather a crime of significant magnitude against the highest authority, conspiring to steal the legitimate owner's position. The original Hebrew text of Genesis 3:5 reads, "Be God" and points out that early English versions added words for sentence structure in our language and translated it "be as gods." There is an ocean of difference between "being as gods" compared to "being God." In God's view, it was not only Grand Theft Garden, it was Grand Theft Throne. Adam and Eve were stealing His position as the owner.

Genesis 3:5 (BBE): "For God sees that on the day when you take of its fruit, your eyes will be open, and you will be as gods, having knowledge of good and evil."

Genesis 3:5 (NET): "For God knows that when you eat from it your eyes will open and you will be like divine beings who know good and evil."

Note the difficulty in translating just two Hebrew words, "hayah" and "elohiym," trying to make them fit English structure. Literal Hebrew is simply "be God." The translators read the whole group of words and form an English sentence. As you see from the huge number of translations available, the work of translating is largely opinion and not science. They try their best to render the true meaning, but exact, word-for-word translation isn't possible in most cases because of the structural difference in the languages. In this case, the meaning would be better served by not adding any English filler words.

By using the two Hebrew words "be God," we get a different meaning than "being like God or as God." It is the difference between just stealing the Garden and stealing the entire throne. To be like God and own the Garden and make its rules is far different than to *be God* and take the throne, the very position of God in the universe. We do tend to think this planet and the entire universe is ours.

Translations are subject to the preset beliefs of the translator. Our human nature leads us to diminish our failures just like Adam and Eve did in the Garden. We have not risen above the standard we inherited from them and struggle to see things from God's view. It is amazing how some of the greatest truths of the Bible have been lost in English because of preset beliefs and cultural differences that filter in through translation bias.

A Similar Historical Case

Isaiah records for us an event that occurred before the Garden crime incident. In chapter fourteen of his Old Testament prophecy, verse twelve begins his narrative of the crime against God perpetrated by Satan. He records the following details of the crime:

Isaiah 14:12–14 (VOICE)

My, how you've fallen from *the heights of* heaven!
O morning star, son of the dawn!
What a star you were, as you *menaced and* weakened the
nations,
but now you've been cut down, *fallen* to earth.
Remember how you said to yourself,
"I will ascend to heaven—*reach higher and with more power*—
and set my throne high above God's own stars?"
Remember how you thought you could be a god, saying:
"I will sit *among them* at the mount of assembly in
the northern heights.
I will rise above the highest clouds and
make myself like the Most High"?

This situation is eerily similar to the events in the Garden. The angel Lucifer, now known as Satan, attempted to take over the realm of the heavens, just as he encouraged Adam and Eve to take over the Garden. The last two Hebrew words translated into the final phrase, "I will be like the most High," are "damah" and "elyon." If you were to attempt to translate "damah" with just one word, you could choose "considered." "Elyon" can be translated with the word "supreme."

The text reveals Lucifer as the first to consider himself an equal supreme being. Is it any wonder that he would tempt Adam and Eve with the same concept, "Make yourself into a God"? It is no surprise then, with that influence and heritage, we live like we own ourselves, as our very own gods. We don't use those words, nor do we like the expression of them. Everyone would deny that they are a god, but in practical living, we live like we are owners. If God is the true owner of everything and everybody, are we not committing the same error as Adam and Eve almost daily?

Reopen the Case without Prejudice

To understand why we as humans fail to comprehend God's basic premise, we must examine what happened in the Garden of Eden. When I became a Christian and read the book of Genesis, the narrative was easy to understand. But I was looking at it through human eyes. I framed the references from all that I knew. I grew up with parents who focused on my behavior. All of us had parents who trained us to do some things and not do others. We grow up learning a straightforward, performance-based view of the world.

The Bible narrative seemed to fit right in, or at least my mind made it fit. Even the statement to Cain in Genesis 4:7, "If you do

well, will you not be accepted," seemed to uphold the behavior-
or works-based view. In reading and studying other writers, Adam
and Eve's failure is usually taught as an act of disobedience, a
behavioral problem. But in fact, Adam and Eve failed because of a
heart issue that led them to question God's authority. That thought
process translated into an act contrary to God's instruction.

In any crime scene, motive or intent is the key issue investigators search for to understand why the event happened. If the crime
scene investigator had a predetermined cause in mind, he will look
for evidence to support that theory. Scholars investigating the
temptation look for a motive that fits their preconceptions. Because
we see scripture through the fixed lens of behavior, we look for a
motive that supports our worldview.

Reexamine the Witness Statements

If we look closely at the serpent's appeal to Adam and Eve, we
see several possibilities. The verse reads as follows: "For God
doth know that in the day ye eat [of that fruit], then your eyes shall
be opened, and ye shall be as gods, knowing good and evil"
(Genesis 3:5). Our normal eyes see the act of eating and the appeal
of knowing good and evil. It is easy to link eating with learning
and pursuing knowledge. That appeals to our flesh and pride.
Who would not like to be smarter than others or even as smart as
God?

Some teach that the serpent appealed to Adam and Eve's pride
of life: improvement of themselves. But that is a possibility viewed
only through our lens. Let's look at another possibility, one far
more complex and deep. If you were to look though God's lens,
the serpent's phrase "be gods" stands out. When you try to replace

God, He takes it personally. In doing so, you challenge God at the core of His being and commit the ultimate in disrespect. Remember, it was not the act of eating the fruit, but the attitude of the heart that offended God.

The Verdict and Sentence Phase

In the Garden, God gave Adam and Eve the opportunity to confess and forsake their newfound rebellion to His ownership. He asked in Genesis 3:11, "Have you eaten of the tree, whereof I commanded that you should not eat?" That was their opportunity to confess and forsake their sin. Proverbs 28:13 reads, "He that covers his sins shall not prosper, but whoso confesses and forsakes them shall have mercy." God is a God of second chances.

They continued to make mistakes and blame the next person in line. When the line is short, blame anything you see around you, but never admit your mistake. Sounds like the last political season. We live in a world of blamers. We are good at blaming others, just as Adam and Eve taught us.

Adam and Eve's sin was not the act, but the attitude. God looked far beyond a disobedient act that could have been punished or corrected with a time-out, or sitting in the corner of the Garden for a few hours or days. God saw the offense through His lens. He saw an attempt to be God, to take His place as owner and rule-maker of the Garden. This was not a behavior issue, but a full-scale rebellion against the order of the universe.

Did you ever have your two-year-old do that? If you don't solve that rebellion at two, you will face it again at thirteen, seventeen, twenty-one, and thirty-five, should you live long enough. Well, Adam and Eve would not take the rebuke and learn from it.

They dodged responsibility, so God evicted them from the Garden. He was not giving up His ownership, so eviction was the only solution. The correction was not made in their lives, so they were driven out only to have the rebellion rise again thirteen years later, five hundred years later, a thousand years later—running up to present times. We still want to be God and own His Garden.

Do you have a deed to your house? Do you think you own it? What if God decides to burn it down? Can you stop Him? Maybe He will just blow it down to prove who the owner of this planet is. Or try not paying your real estate taxes and see who comes to take it from you. Are you certain you own it?

Thou Shalt Surely Die (Genesis 2:17)

God determined the punishment He imposed on Adam and Eve. God separated Himself from them. He drove them out of the Garden. He stopped providing for them. They would now have to work by the sweat of their brow to provide for themselves. He sent weeds into their fields and pain into the birth process. But He did not stop there. He had previously warned them of imminent death.

Death to the Spirit

The moment they tried to become owners like God, a spiritual death occurred. That death separated them from God. They had been created in the image of God as a trinity: body, soul, and spirit. Their spirit, that compartment in them that contained the breath of God, died to His presence immediately. That spiritual death was the result of the entrance of evil into mankind. NOW, they saw nakedness. They had already known the good. All they'd discovered was the evil and how different it was from the good.

Since Adam's spiritual demise, all his descendants are born spiritually dead. You can't pass on something you don't have. We come into this world without life in our spirit. We still have a spirit because we are a trinity, but it is an empty spiritual compartment with a propensity toward evil. We must be taught to do good. We pick up bad behaviors and attitudes on our own. The cure for that dead spirit was explained to Nicodemus in John 3:3 (NCV) when Jesus said, "I tell you the truth, unless you are born again, you cannot be in God's presence."

Death to the Soul

Being a trinity, we also died immediately in our soul. For it is in the soul, the mind of man, that evil was now present and became his preeminent thought pattern. Selfishness, pride, self-centeredness, judgment, and criticism have become normal thought patterns. Our twisted minds pursue whatever is in our own best interest to own or control our world. Scripture records God's evaluation of our mental state:

Genesis 6:5

And GOD saw that the wickedness of man was
great in the earth,
and that every imagination of the thoughts of his
heart was only evil continually.

Jeremiah 17:9

The heart is deceitful above all things,
and desperately wicked: who can know it?

We see the first evidence of this mental demise in the desire of Adam and Eve to find covering for their bodies. Now, after the death of their mental state, they knew evil thinking. Not being able to stop the evil thoughts, they had to find another way to control the cerebral carnage. External things like fig leaves became essential to covering the problem.

Death to the Body

Besides the deaths of the spirit and the mind, a physical death also occurred. This death is more of a slow process that ages and degenerates us over time, but it began right there in the garden. Sin kills our body's cells. They no longer function perfectly. During cell division, our DNA does not always reproduce perfectly. The ends of the DNA break off or do not reproduce to the full extent, so our genetics are in decline. That is the aging process our dying bodies go through every day. Cells no longer have the same vibrancy and life they had when we were born. They no longer function or look as good as they once did.

Out of God's mercy, death was made a gradual process rather than something immediate. But nonetheless, it began at the moment of sin. The process of death had begun and was imminent. God announced the outcome of the process:

Genesis 3:19

In the sweat of thy face shalt thou eat bread,

till thou return unto the ground;

for out of it wast thou taken:

for dust thou art, and unto dust shalt thou return.

CHAPTER 13

JOURNEY THROUGH
THE WILDERNESS

The Wilderness Journey Is an Archetype for Our Instruction

1 Corinthians 10:5–6 (MKJV)
But with many of them God was not well pleased,
for they were scattered in the wilderness.
And these things were our examples . . .

The Old Testament journey of the Israelites from Egypt to the Promised Land is an interesting story when seen as a whole. We often study it in parts because it is spread over six books of the Bible. It begins in Genesis with the Israelites going to Egypt to avoid a famine and ends in the book of Joshua with the crossing of the Jordan River into the Promised Land.

It is a journey from slavery to freedom, from being owned by someone else to the claiming of a great inheritance. It is the travail of building structures for the Egyptian masters to possessing a land with wells dug by other people. It is the progress from captivity to the abundance of a land flowing with milk and honey. If we take the journey with them from a vantage point well above the map of the area, we can see what God is doing in their struggle that reflects our spiritual journey.

The Physical Journey Summarized

We pick up the story in Egypt where the children of Jacob, now called Israel, have multiplied over four hundred years to become a national identity of their own. During those years, the host nation of Egypt sought to control the Israelites by enslaving them. As the duties of the slaves became severe and their treatment grievous, Moses came on the scene to deliver the people and lead them back to the land they had left four centuries before. Moses would lead them to the Promised Land, so called because God had promised Abraham it would be the homeland of his descendants.

Moses struggled to free the people from the Egyptian pharaoh. With God's help, he performed powerful miracles to demonstrate God's power and demand their freedom. Once the people were free to go, Moses raised his staff and God parted the Red Sea. The Israelites crossed on dry land, but the entire Egyptian army drowned when they tried to pursue them.

After crossing into the Sinai Peninsula, Moses brought the people to Mount Sinai. There on top of the mountain, God gave Moses the Ten Commandments written in stone. After camping near the mountain to build a temporary tabernacle, the Israelites traveled north to Kadesh on the southern edge of the Promised Land. They sent in twelve spies to evaluate the local inhabitants. Ten of the spies came back with a bad report describing giants too formidable to defeat. Two spies saw the battle as winnable.

Fearing the giants, the people revolted and refused to enter the Promised Land. They erroneously surmised that the battle was theirs to win and not God's. They forgot the awesome victory they had just witnessed at the Red Sea where God alone had fought for them and destroyed an entire army without having to lift a sword. Because of their failure to believe in His promise to fight for them, God directed them to stay in the wilderness until a generation had passed. He would lead the next generation who possessed more faith and trust in the Lord to victory in the Promised Land.

Forty years passed. Now they were being led by Joshua on the banks of the Jordan River to attempt once again to enter the land. They again sent in spies to survey what they were up against as they contemplated the battle ahead. In Jericho, the spies met the woman Rahab, who asked them a pointed question: "Where have you been for forty years? We were ready to run from you and your God the minute you entered our area. We had heard how your God had destroyed the largest army in the world, the Egyptian army by drowning them in the Red Sea. We were too afraid to fight against your God" (Joshua 2:9–11). Her statement made it clear that the victory could have been won forty years earlier, if only they would have had the faith to walk in and claim it.

The first battle in the Promised Land was at Jericho, just three miles from the Jordan River. There, the Israelites marched around the city seven times and the walls of the city fell. A few generations later, a boy named David went back to the Kadesh area to defeat one of the giants, named Goliath. David killed him easily with a mere slingshot. Giants may seem large to us, but in God's view, they are just minor obstacles of no consequence.

Their Physical Journey Compared to Our Spiritual Journey

The exodus from Egypt and journey into the wilderness is a migration from a land owned by the evil one to a land owned by God, the Promised Land. The wilderness between those two contrasting lands marks the area where we have broken free of the ownership of the powers of darkness, but have not yet learned to give ownership over to God. After leaving the lost world to travel the wilderness, we still live as though we are owners. This middle ground is where we struggle to increase our faith and trust in God preparing us for the Promised Land, where we allow Him full ownership of our life. Living in the Promised Land is like living back in the Garden where God is owner and rule-maker.

Egypt is a representative of the world apart from God that binds all of us in a sinful, destructive way of life, controlled and owned by the prince and power of the air, the devil. The crossing of the Red Sea represents our decision to leave the world of sin behind and follow Jesus. Those in Egypt are following the world and its systems. Those who cross the Red Sea into the Sinai Peninsula are those who follow Jesus and believe that He is the Messiah who died on the cross as payment for sin.

When you accept the gift of salvation provided by His substitutionary sacrifice, your path as a believer takes you through a time of learning and growing. That journey is a type of Sinai experience on our way to learning what God intends for our spiritual goal, our Promised Land. We need to take the time around Mount

Sinai, the Ten Commandments, as we begin to clean the outside appearance of how we live our lives. We have some things we no longer want to do, and we begin some new quests that take us in a godlier direction. We match the standards of the denomination or church we are attending by putting down those things that distract us and focusing our attention on directions given to us by our fellow believers.

We shed the things of the past life as we advance toward the coming Place of Rest, our spiritual Promised Land. We are not talking about heaven, the place we go after death. We are specifically looking at the spiritual level God wants us to function in while we are still here on this earth.

Soon enough, we all must face the giant, which is the truth that God wants ALL of us, not just a portion of our life. Can we give God our all? Can He be our owner, our controller, our very life so He can use us as He chooses? It is a gigantic decision. How much of myself will I keep and how much will I give to God? That is a frightening giant to face since until now we have been in control of our own lives. A few may make it into the life He has for us by defeating the giant right there, giving everything to Jesus. But the vast majority are unable to win that battle over the flaw of self-ownership we were born with.

Most go on to dwell in the wilderness of Christian life still in control, still owning and controlling our own lives. We ask for God's help. We're happy to give Him management-level status in our lives, but fall short of giving Him ownership. We are routinely in control of our own lives and activities. We like making our own decisions and directing our own lives. To surrender ownership of ourselves to God is a giant we can't easily defeat.

We are unaware that the battle is already won, and living in the Place of Rest is a much better life than we could ever have in the wilderness of Christian efforts and self-direction. All we must do to obtain the Place of Rest is walk into it, a monumental choice. Submit to His ownership and you will see and feel the victories. You only need the confidence to take the steps to follow Him. We often fail to walk into God's total ownership of our lives because we cannot see that He will take better care of us than we ever could. Another reason we fail is our lack of understanding of the vision God has put before us. Many fail to see that a Place of Rest exists.

Because of our unbelief, we fail to enter the Place of Rest, our Promised Land, the Abundant Life. We fail to believe what God provides is better than what we have now. We doom ourselves to the Christian wilderness of self-control and self-government. We ask for God's help in our lives rather than offering our lives to Him. We want Him to help our cause while we remain the owner. We are still being God in the sense we own our lives and only surrender management or an assistant position to God. We do not offer him total ownership.

We will live in the wilderness until we get sick of the failures we bring upon ourselves. Only when our failures and tragedies become so great do we seek a way for God to take over. It seems a generation or a major part of our life must pass before we find a new way into the Place of Rest. When we realize our own baggage from the past is destroying us, we finally give it to God and stumble across the Jordan River into our Place of Rest. We cross into the Place of Rest over a bridge called Forgiveness. This is where we find it easiest to let God own a small part our life. We are willing, by way of forgiving, to let God own the baggage of our past.

The Israelites spent forty years in the wilderness; we may spend that much time or more in our own wilderness. Many fall and die in the Christian wilderness of self-ownership. It is the time and place where we own our lives and remain in control. We are the final decision maker because we are the owner. Far too many Christians live in this middle ground and never reach the Place of Rest. They die still in the sin of Adam, thinking they own something that does not belong to them.

Summary of Our Spiritual Journey

It is far better to be in the wilderness than back in Egypt lost in sin. Just as God fed the Israelites manna from heaven, so do we get spiritual feasts from God in our wilderness journey. We can be blind to the fact that we are still carrying a great deal of our original problem, the desire to own. Many cannot see that there is yet ahead a Place of Rest where God is allowed to be the owner.

Some believers learn so much in the wilderness, they feel they have arrived. Others feel they have arrived because they get so much wealth, or so many blessings, or spiritual anointing. There are groups located right on the Red Sea that major in attracting the lost from Egypt over to the Christian side. Some have mansions on the seashore with great views, satisfied with the level they have achieved or feeling anointed or elected by God to enjoy their possessions.

Some are located near Mount Sinai, where they concentrate on the laws and are very judgmental. They analyze the words of the Bible and judge others for not upholding the minute points they deem essential. They set the standard that only they meet. They stay close to Mount Sinai and never move on to Kadesh near the edge of the Place of Rest. They concentrate on learning and going deeper in Bible knowledge.

Still others are led astray deeper into the wilderness because they have been distracted. The diversion may be a doctrine they stand on and champion that puts them above the simple exhortation to follow. They may pursue something that leads to human pride because they feel they have a superior knowledge. Still others are distracted by following a person or dynamic leader rather than Jesus. He said, "Follow Me," not "follow my followers." In fact, he warned us about those who might lead us away from Jesus and toward their own agendas. These false leaders love praise and want a following. They want to be God by stealing His glory, the praise that only He deserves. Matthew records in 7:15, "Beware of false prophets, which come to you in sheep's clothing, but inwardly they are ravening wolves."

Any group located on the banks of the Jordan River will help you cross the river into the Promised Land. They are a forgiving people that model unconditional forgiveness. They help others turn the baggage weighing them down over to God so that He can own and carry those burdens. When a loss is suffered, they hold a forgiving service, giving the hurt to God. It carries each of them across the Jordan to the other side where God owns a part of them—their baggage. Once in the Place of Rest, they experience the peace of God that passes all understanding. They look around and let God own more and more so they can stay in His Place of Rest.

Most of us must cross the shallow waters of the Jordan rather than take on the big fight at Kadesh. At the Jordan, we find it easy to give God ownership of the one thing that is destroying us—

our baggage. If we fail to give up ownership of the baggage, we are doomed by the load of bitterness in our heart to stay in the Christian wilderness until we die there in our sins.

The Garden of Eden, the Promised Land, and the Place of Rest are all owned by God. They are the spiritual dwelling places for those who have declared God their owner. The Garden is now closed. The Promised Land is for the Israelites. We can access our Place of Rest by giving God ownership of some of our life. It will take us across the Jordan into the Land of Milk and Honey, but we will soon run into our very own Jericho, where we will face things we still must give over to God. You only stay in the Place of Rest by giving God ownership of everything.

As the Israelites marched around Jericho seven times, so we will journey through several more stages that lead us to give over ownership of all areas of our lives. Once we have tasted the peace of our Place of Rest and see how well God handles small things, we let him own more and more of our lives. God owns everything in the Place of Rest, so not getting evicted is a matter of growing and letting God take over ownership of every area of our lives.

CHAPTER 14

FOUNDATIONS
IN SCRIPTURE

Thine—An Ownership Word—It Belongs to HIM

Matthew 6:13b

For thine is the kingdom, and the power, and the
glory, for ever.

1 Chronicles 29:11

Thine, O LORD is the greatness, and the power,
and the glory, and the victory, and the majesty:
for all that is in the heaven and in the earth is thine;
thine is the kingdom, O LORD,
and thou art exalted as head above all.

The Lord's Prayer as recorded in Matthew 6 ends in a phrase that is a truth drawn from David's prayer in 1 Chronicles 29:11. Jesus often quoted from the Old Testament. Here, he concludes his model prayer with this profound statement: "for thine is the kingdom, power, and glory."

The phrase begins with the word "for." It is a foundation word. When you see the word "for," you look at what preceded it. The previous lines or statements have put the structure together and framed the building. All the structure we just built or the words we just used are solidly grounded because of the foundation that is going to be brought into focus. All the previous lines of the prayer are good and work well because of this great truth—He is the owner.

I have heard many speak about and quote the Lord's Prayer. When the last phrase is addressed, what stands out are the words kingdom, glory, and power. The word "thine" is glossed over and not emphasized. Our limited foresight and self-centered views of the world and the Bible distract us from God's perspective. To God, the most important word is "thine." It is an ownership word. It is His kingdom. We talk about and discuss the kingdom and declare our membership in it based on our faith in Jesus. We think and act as if we have a share in its bounty and abundance. We fail to see the word "thine" in all its significance. It is all His; everything is His.

Realizing this, "thine" becomes the most important word in the whole prayer. Every declaration, request, petition, and precept rests on its wide base. Because He is the owner—hallowed be His name. Because He is the owner—thy Kingdom shall come. Because He is the owner—thy will shall be done in heaven and on earth. Because He is the owner—we forgive our offenders and debts because they belong to God in the first place. We should not have tried to own them. Because He is the owner—we plead with Him to not test us, knowing our poor success record. Because He is the owner—we need His power to help us avoid evil. It is all built on His ownership.

Some of the newer translations omit this phrase from the Lord's Prayer. They offer no proof that the phrase was not given by Jesus, only their human logic of how they think it may have been added by someone later as a footnote. It is only important to know that the truth of the phrase is listed already in the Old Testament and that Jesus often quoted Old Testament scriptures.

Those that diminish this phrase may find themselves on the wrong side of the human war we wage against God and His position as owner. Ownership is the root cause of man's and the devil's failure. I can understand man's effort as well as the devil's to try to get that phrase erased from man's mind, memory, and from the Bible. The word of God stands forever. Do not minimize this phase containing this truth. You will see this truth again when you stand before God. The assertion of this truth is listed too many times in the scripture to be taken lightly. I remind those who would diminish scripture for their own intellectual glory, who try to shed light on their brilliance rather than the truth of God, that they are not eyewitnesses to God's inspiration; therefore, they cannot judge properly or absolutely.

Against Thee Only

Psalm 51:4

Against thee, thee only, have I sinned, and done this
evil in thy sight:

that thou mightest be justified when thou speakest,

and be clear when thou judgest.

The underlying truth of God's ownership is given above. David claims all sin is against God and Him alone. What a profound, extreme position to declare. We need to examine this verse carefully, because the truth it contains proves once and for all who owns us—ourselves or God?

This truth goes against our very nature. When we are offended, we conclude that the offender has sinned against us and owes us an apology. Even the offender would agree that the intent was to injure you, not God. The last thing an offender wants is God coming after him or getting revenge for what he has done. The offender tramples over you because he intends to hurt you or at least to get some gain for himself, with you being collateral damage.

We need to get a clear picture of our relationship we have with the things we own. Let's pick something we own and evaluate our interaction with that property. I will use a car for this illustration.

As the owner of a car, I am responsible for everything about that car. I may not know how to tune the engine or change a flat tire, but I am responsible for having someone do the work and for paying for that work. When the car stops running or breaks down, no one cares except me. Until the owner is ready to pay for the repair or do the repair himself, the car will sit unused.

If I damage someone else's car, I owe the owner for the damage I inflicted on his property. I would not pay the car for the damage; I would pay the owner of the car. The car does not pay for its repair; it depends on the owner to do that. The car would sit and wait with no repair because the owner is responsible, not the car. So, all damage to the car by someone else is owed to the owner of the car. The money for the damage is not split. You don't give 90 percent to the owner and 10 percent to the car, even if the car said "ouch" when you hit it. It gets nothing for pain and suffering. The owner gets all the money. He can keep the money and junk the car, or he may fix it. He will do whatever he wishes with the car.

So it is with the truth of Psalm 51:4. All damages done to us are to be paid to the owner of the person injured. That owner is God and the value of the damage is to be paid to Him. Even if we felt the damage, 100 percent of the damage is owed to God and Him alone. If God is the owner, we don't get 10 percent for pain and suffering. If one owns themselves, then the apology or value of the damage could be demanded by that party. But David makes it clear that 100 percent is due to God. That makes Him 100 percent owner.

He goes on to give the ramifications of God's ownership. God has total freedom to judge and be justified or correct in that judgment against offenders. If I owned even just 10 percent of myself, God would have to ask me if the payment He was inflicting against the perpetrator was acceptable and satisfied my 10 percent interest. I would have a say in the judgment rendered. But because God is 100 percent the owner, He is free and just to demand whatever He needs to satisfy the demands of the offense without input from me.

Thank God when I make a mistake, God is my judge, and not men. Men have very little mercy. It is also worthy to note the warning that goes with God's ownership; there is no escape or easy way out by thinking you can fool the judge or hide anything from Him.

All Claims under Heaven

Job 41:11 (GW)

Who can confront me that I should repay him?
Everything under heaven belongs to me!

1 Chronicles 29:14 (CEV)

But why should we be happy that we have given
you these gifts?
They belong to you, and we have only given back
what is already yours.

How far out does heaven begin? Where is the throne of God? Somewhere in space is God's demarcation where earth and its atmospheric heavens constitute our boundaries and His heaven begins. That limit must be beyond the limits of our travel. No man will ever get into the heavens so high he can claim not to belong to God. The author (Luke) of the book of Acts tells us in 17:26 that God has set a limit on our boundaries. Only man's imagination takes him out of God's reach. Reality trumps imagination. Our universe is God's backyard.

Genesis teaches us God created the heavens and the earth. We view the heavens as far as our telescopes can reach. All that space, God created with the sound of his voice. With another word, all matter was created and scattered into the space. And then God said, "Let there be light." With those words, time was created. Light is a moving wave of energy. For it to move there must be time, because at one moment it is here, and the next moment it is somewhere else. It is time that separates those two places. Therefore,

God existed before time; He existed before space and matter. Because He is the creator of time, space, and matter, He is not bound by them but functions above and beyond them. We will forever be in awe of our God when we can see or comprehend Him in His power and glory. We will appear small and foolish for ever doubting Him or thinking of taking His place.

God asks Job, "To whom do I owe anything?" If God owns everything, nothing is owed to anyone but God. If you gave God something, what have you given Him? Just something he already owned. So do not boast that you have given to God. You have only returned things He had previously loaned to you.

With God's position as owner in mind, we can understand the followers of Jesus in Acts 2:44–45 as they "sold all their possessions and goods and parted them to the believers and had all things in common." First-century believers had a better understanding and far more passion than exists today. Everything was God's, and Jesus had just purchased them back a second time. They had no problem giving everything they had to God, because He had just given His only begotten Son for them. They could not keep back what already belonged to God.

And if something is taken from you, how can you make a claim that it should be paid back to you? Everything that was taken belonged to God, not you. You had no legal claim to keep whatever was taken, even intangible things like dignity and respect.

Who are you aside from God? James, the brother of Jesus, said in James 4:14, "For what is your life? It is even a vapour that appeareth for a little time, and then vanisheth away." By making ourselves owners in our own mind, we give ourselves ownership rights. It is difficult to address the topic of pride. It is so ingrained in us, we cannot imagine what the Garden of Eden was like before human pride destroyed the peace associated with devotion to God in humility.

All Claims in the Heavens

Genesis 1:1

In the beginning God created the heaven and the earth.

Psalm 8:3

When I consider thy heavens, the work of thy fingers,
the moon and the stars, which thou hast ordained . . .

Psalm 19:1

The heavens declare the glory of God;
and the firmament showeth his handywork.

The stars, moon, sun, and all the heavens were created by God, so they are His. When you consider the immense universe, you must stand in awe of the God who created it.

When I was a young boy, long before the Hubble Space Telescope, I would lie on my back in the yard at night and gaze at the stars. Far in the country, away from city lights, the sky was ablaze with stars. What an amazing sight that our modern cities have obliterated with the streetlights, making it impossible for so many to see the full magnitude of the host of stars.

The space optics we now have allowed us to get above the distortion caused by our atmosphere. Now we can see stars without the twinkle that our atmosphere produces as light travels through it. The stars appear much smaller to the Hubble Telescope. The twinkle makes them appear larger to us and therefore visible to the naked eye.

But when the Hubble trains its lens on a cluster of what we saw as stars, it sees them clearly as galaxies. The number of galaxies can only be estimated. They cannot yet be counted. The number of stars in each galaxy also can only be approximated. And God made all of this. He owns every star and can call them by name. If He was trying to impress us with a billboard in the sky, I think He more than accomplished His goal. The God who made the heavens is not a God to be taken lightly. He is not a God you should try to step in front of or assume you can be. Being God by thinking we own what He made is arrogance beyond measure. What fools we can be!

The World and Its People

Psalm 24:1 (CEV)

The earth and everything on it belong to the LORD.
The world and its people belong to him.

The scope of this verse leaves no room for exceptions. Can you put your mind around the entire earth belonging to God and every person on the planet? It is not just the Garden of Eden that belonged to God, but the wilderness he banished mankind to occupy after the Garden also belonged to Him. He allocated an area He owns so we could go live as we please, as far away from God as we decided to venture. But He still owns it. He is still responsible, which means He is still the judge and final decision maker for all that happens on the whole planet. Just because we have turned our back on God and pretend to imagine He doesn't exist doesn't mean He isn't there when we open our eyes and ears enough to see the truth.

He owns every single person. It does not matter if you damage a good or a bad person, a religious or a nonreligious person, a Greek or a Roman, a Jew or a Gentile—you will owe God for that damage because He owns them all. There is no deed or word that does not come under His jurisdiction.

Please note, if you harm yourself, you will answer to your owner as well. Man was created in the image of God with a body, soul, and spirit. The biggest enemy we have is ourselves. For the most part, with a few exceptions, we damage ourselves more than any other person on the planet. We destroy ourselves with negative, evil, and selfish thoughts. No one hurts you as much as you hurt yourself. Put your mind on God instead of yourself. Isaiah gave us a role model to strive for when he directed us with these words from Isaiah 26:3: "Thou wilt keep him in perfect peace, whose mind is stayed on thee." Our own destruction is sown in our own thoughts as outlined by David in Psalm 2:1 (NLV) with this phrase: "Why are the nations so shaken up and the people planning foolish things?" Our thoughts are too much about ourselves and not enough about God.

The Pasture Land and the Sheep

Psalm 100:3 (CEV)
You know the LORD is God!
He created us, and we belong to him;
we are his people, the sheep in his pasture.

In our world as we understand it, if one invents or creates something, they are the natural owner of that item until they sell it or give it away. An item may become lost, but ownership does not change. The creator or manufacturer will search for that item so it can be returned to inventory and put in its rightful place. Since God created us, He owns us.

There is no record that would indicate God has sold or given away His claim to anyone on the planet. He may have given them space to pursue their reprobate minds or get as far from Him as they could, but ownership never changed. They may have been lost or wandered far away, but He still searches for them. God's ownership is displayed in Luke 19:10: "For the Son of man is come to seek and to save that which was lost." Though one is far away from God, he still belongs to the creator.

As the owner, He still retains the right to dispose of the property the way He sees fit, hence the judgment. No one will ever claim God does not have authority to judge them because they belong to another jurisdiction. There is no escape from the one who created you. Only the owner can determine when to repair or junk the item. One day, the nations of this earth will answer to the real owner of their realm. The apostle John revealed in Revelation 10:6 that a time will arrive when God will no longer loan out His earth to us, but will take possession back. John put it this way:

Revelation 10:6–7

And sware by him that liveth for ever and ever, who
created heaven,
and the things that therein are, and the earth,
and the things that therein are, and the sea, and the

> things which are therein,
> that there should be time no longer:
> But in the days of the voice of the seventh angel,
> when he shall begin to sound,
> the mystery of God should be finished . . .

The mystery John mentions is only a mystery to us, not to God. God has put the descendants of Adam on notice; time is running out on our blindness and willful ignorance of the God who owns us. We have been placed here to tend God's Garden, not to own it. There will come the day we give up possession of this earth and hand it over to God. The real owner is God. Have we ever admitted that truth? We will explore the mystery of God in the conclusion of the book.

The Redeemed—Owned a Second Time—Purchased Back

1 Corinthians 6:20

> For ye are bought with a price: therefore glorify
> God in your body,
> and in your spirit, which are God's.

God owns us twice over. Not only did He create us, but He purchased us a second time. When we left His protective shelter to take control and attempt to own ourselves, He paid the price of redemption, shedding the blood of His Son that we might have an avenue back to His presence. Without God providing the means of return, we had no passageway to Him.

It is not just a path back He provided; He purchased us and paid the price to free us from the penalty of our rebellion. We were held for ransom by the sheer weight of our sins against the judgment to come. He paid that price to set us free to begin our journey back to Him.

That is the real story of God's love. The apostle John gave us the summary of the message contained in the scripture when he wrote the following words in John 3:16: "For God so loved the world, that he gave his only begotten Son, that whosoever believeth in him should not perish, but have everlasting life."

CHAPTER 15

TEXT MESSAGE
FROM HEAVEN

Luke 6:37

Judge not, and ye shall not be judged:

condemn not, and ye shall not be condemned:

forgive, and ye shall be forgiven . . .

Christianity is based on the resurrection of Jesus. The resurrection is the central part of what made the followers of Jesus fervent and dedicated. It is central to the message they carried forth across the globe and into our time. The apostle Paul highlights this truth in his first letter to the Corinthians, writing in 15:3–4 (CEV), "I told you the most important part of the message exactly as it was told to me. That part is: Christ died for our sins, as the Scriptures say. He was buried, and three days later he was raised to life, as the Scriptures say." The resurrection is the capstone of the message of Jesus.

The resurrection was also proof that God had accepted the sacrifice Jesus offered for the sins of the world. John points out the scope of the payment for sin when he wrote 1 John 2:2 (CEV), "Christ is the sacrifice that takes away our sins and the sins of all the world's people." Without the resurrection, Christianity would have died or have been just one more religious system. Paul points out in 1 Corinthians 15:14, "And if Christ be not risen, then is our preaching vain, and your faith is also vain."

The need for a sacrifice is based on the need for sins to be forgiven. Since mankind has rebelled against God's ownership and authority from the beginning, the scriptures have foretold how God would have to provide a way of reconciliation because mankind could not come back on their own merits.

Paul summarizes the need we had in his letter when he wrote Romans 3:23–25 (MSG):

> Since we've compiled this long and sorry record as
> sinners (both us and them)
> and proved that we are utterly incapable of living
> the glorious lives God wills for us
> [not capable of earning salvation] God did it for us.
> Out of sheer generosity he put us in right standing
> with himself. A pure gift.
> He got us out of the mess we're in and restored us
> to where he always wanted us to be.
> And he did it by means of Jesus Christ. God
> sacrificed Jesus on the altar of the world
> to clear that world of sin. Having faith in him sets
> us in the clear.

God decided on this course of action in full view of
the public—
to set the world in the clear with himself through
the sacrifice of Jesus,
finally taking care of the sins he had so patiently endured.

Christianity is built around the topic of forgiveness constructed on the foundation of the sacrificial death and resurrection of Jesus. So, Christians should find the truth about being forgiven easy to understand and follow. Forgiving is the bottom line to our faith. It is what we ask of God to do for us, and what God asks of us to do for Him. We forgive because we have been forgiven. The epistle to the Ephesians records it this way in 4:32 (MSG): "Forgive one another as quickly and thoroughly as God in Christ forgave you." The followers of Jesus should understand this truth easily.

Hard Road for the Natural Human

Those that are not depending on God's grace given in Jesus, but rather consider themselves as not needing a savior, have a more difficult time in learning to forgive. They operate without the trust or lessons provided in Jesus and must master forgiveness in their own strength. The principles of forgiveness to bring peace to a life are effective for any who will learn to forgive.

Forgiveness is a major underlying truth taught in Hinduism and Buddhism. Humans have learned across the world that holding grudges is harmful to your health and life. It's no surprise that people of other faiths and those who hold to no faith still find forgiveness an important part of a healthy or a spiritual life.

Forgiveness is within their reach. Forgiving is not an impossible task outside of a faith in Jesus. It is just harder in my view. It takes more determination and strength because you are accomplishing the task without God's help. You go at it alone or with the example of other humans. Gandhi and Buddha practiced forgiving and taught it to their followers.

People have developed a management system through counselors to help cope with their past and forgive. Most secular counseling is based on digging into your past to find those events your mind has hidden so that the patient can rethink through them and deal with them. Usually the solution is forgiving oneself for what happened or forgiving the offenders. Generally, Christian counselors aim at forgiving the other party. Secular counselors tend to target coping mechanisms and reevaluation or forgiving of the individual themselves. They can spend many hours with a client in psychoanalysis digging through memories that have been hidden.

There is a lot of material available on the topic of forgiving. If a person searches the Internet for "forgive," "forgiving," "forgiving instantly," and "forgiveness," they will find books and quotes that people have devised as management tools to help convince one to forgive. There are hundreds of quotes that people have generated over time to help them see the value of forgiving and the cost of not forgiving.

The book *Forgive Instantly & Live Free* uses the words and principle Jesus gave in the Sermon on the Mount to outline the cure for life's dysfunctions. For those willing to follow Jesus, forgiving is the great path to the Abundant Life. I am grateful that the book made His message easy to understand.

Too many Christians harbor hard feelings, display anger and frustrations, criticize, argue, and exhibit all manner of dysfunctions because they will not forgive. We appear to the outside world as no different when we are unable to display peace, calm, and forgiveness. When you come to Jesus, try to find a life of forgiving as fast as you can. You will be taking your first steps into the Place of Rest by letting Him own a few things you really want to get rid of.

Those Who Refuse to Forgive (My Way or the Highway)

There are two groups who refuse to forgive. They are the non-religious folks who hate so much and want to get even so badly that they would rather die than give way to reason. The other group is the religious folks who also hold fast to control and ownership of God's things, even if they must die in their sin.

We can only encourage the first group of nonreligious folks to learn and grow. We can show them the benefits of forgiving, and certainly the benefits of being forgiven. We can show them Jesus and how He has provided forgiveness to them. All they need do is accept it, believe it, and say thank you to the Savior that provided it. The best way to help them is to bring them to Jesus. He can help them better than man-made management tools that we use to cope with our dysfunctions.

The second group of religious people is much harder to work with, if not impossible. Once a jaw is locked into a way of thinking, it is hard to let go, admit the error, and turn to follow the Savior. The Pharisees of the New Testament were set in their ways and were willing to kill to stay on that path they had chosen rather than humble themselves to God. Not even Jesus could reason with them.

Lockjaw is the common name for tetanus and is the result of the toxins released from a common bacterium found around the world. It is an infectious disease of the central nervous system. Since your brain is the control unit of your central nervous system, lockjaw is a fitting description of Christians who are so infected with controlling God, the Bible, and other people that they will die before letting go of their stronghold.

They are owners of the sacred text, and only they can tell you how to live the Christian life. They are the religious elite who think knowing is better than following. They are spoken of by James in 4:11 (GW): "If you judge God's teachings, you are no longer following them. Instead, you are judging them."

Strongholds—Judges, Not Followers

These groups of Christians teach that forgiveness is conditional. They advocate not forgiving until the offender repents and apologizes. They mix verses about reconciliation and church discipline with those of forgiving. It is an easy mistake to make because we gravitate toward any interpretation that gives us more control and ownership. In our humanity, we can easily fail to see the things that led us to God's ownership. This group judges and decides to what degree someone must repent.

John in 3:16 tells us, "God so loved the world, that he gave his only begotten Son, that whosoever believeth in him should not perish, but have everlasting life." When you make a turn in your life, even so simple as deciding to believe in Jesus, you are turning from sin. That turn is a repenting of the old direction. You would not have to move at all—just the fact that you turned around to face the other way is progress.

If you face one direction, you have your back to the other direction. So it is with Jesus. Just turning toward Him is turning your back on evil. The progress of your growth in that direction is up to you and the Holy Spirit, who will guide you personally in your own journey. It is not our job as fellow Christians to point out faults or sins in someone and take on the Holy Spirit's job. The Holy Spirit convicts people of sin. We are being God when we become judgmental of others and expect repentance in some monumental way that we can measure. God looks at the heart; man looks at the exterior.

We need to take ourselves out of the role of being God by requiring the turn or repentance an individual makes be so large that we can measure it. Those who use the verses in the Bible that say, "Repent and believe" are putting their own definition to the word repent. There are many different levels of repentance. Every Christian grows at his own rate. Some make huge changes in measurable, visible ways, but others grow slowly, having made a turn toward Jesus; they are responsible for their own growth. The "conditional-only" forgiveness people are not responsible for growing others. They are simply busybody critics who need to mind their own business. And note, it is not the new Christian's business they are minding; it is God's business they are meddling in. They are being God by judging.

Oh, fellow Christians, can you see the hypocrisy here? We are not to be judges ever. God never gave us that responsibility. Judgmental Christians will always be in a works-based form of Christianity. You will find they themselves are on a works- or behavior-based relationship with Jesus and imposing that same self-effort-based philosophy of Christianity on newcomers. They may claim to be "salvation by grace" followers, but in practice they have subtly imposed human effort after the conversion experience.

Humans are so self-centered; it is so easy for us to step into God's role.

Jesus sees the heart. The turn toward him is a turn away from evil. There is a long journey ahead for those who grow slowly, but it is their journey. Encourage and help them, but do not condemn nor judge them. God is quite capable of convicting of sin or faults. Stop being God by doing a job that belongs to God. Encourage them and advise them, even mention areas to improve in, but never judge.

Those who deny the clear call of Jesus for us to be unconditionally forgiving are the lockjaw Christians of our day. They will certainly never find God's Place of Rest, our Promised Land. They are too busy filling in for God, taking over His power and position. They cannot see how judgmental they are. They are blind to their own self-righteousness.

Limiting the Power of God

Conditional forgiveness folks tend to be those who believe in a limited atonement; Jesus only died for the sins of his followers, not the sins of the whole world. They teach He did not die for, nor did He provide payment for, the sins of those who reject Jesus. In so teaching and placing themselves in a group they call the elect, they limit the forgiving power of God. It is a dangerous thing to limit God, even in your mind.

If you believe that the forgiveness Jesus extends toward mankind is limited, it is easy to make the jump to believing that you should limit the forgiveness you extend toward others. The apostle John, the apostle closest to Jesus, made clear in his first epistle to the church when he said in 1 John 2:2, "And he is the propitiation [payment] for our sins: and not for ours only, but also for the sins of the whole world." If you make a mistake on a fundamental doctrine, more mistakes will follow. Pride leads us to think more highly of ourselves than we ought (Romans 12:3). In that high-mindedness, we miss God's best for us.

Our desire for ownership draws us toward beliefs that simultaneously exalt ourselves and lower God. Anything that will give us power over another is within our capacity. I know these words I write will draw fiery darts, but brethren, consider: is it possible that you are not always right? Is it possible that God is so far ahead of us, we have trouble seeing Him as He is? Has our human view of this world clouded our view of God and who He is? Can we really know God if we filter scriptures as judges? Are we being God by judging?

At least take a "wait and see" attitude. Wait until you get to heaven and hear it from the lips of Jesus before you decide here on this earth that He did not provide salvation for all. I am not saying all will receive Jesus and be in heaven. I am simply saying what John said, which is that Jesus made it available for all if only they receive it by believing.

The summary of the entire Bible is given in John 3:16:

For God so loved the world,
that he gave his only begotten Son,
that whosoever believeth in him should not perish,
but have everlasting life.

Just Take It

The best way I can illustrate the apostle John's message is to use an analogy. Suppose we have a merry-go-round big enough to put every person in the world on it. Just next to the wheel is a souvenir dispenser of brass rings that pops up another ring every time somebody takes one. It is a never-ending supply of brass rings ready for the taking, one at a time, as the riders pass by.

Riders may pass a few times and not notice the ring is there. Some riders are too busy talking or fiddling with something to even notice the ring is available. They exit the ride at the end and have no ring to keep. Some riders see the ring, but don't bother to take one because they think it is something they don't need. They go home without a ring. Some may grab a ring, examine it, and lay it down as something that is not valuable enough to take up space in their pocket or purse. They leave it behind and go home without a ring. But some notice the ring, see its value, and eventually grab the ring, keep it, and take it home as a souvenir.

Salvation in Christ is the same. The ring of salvation is there for everyone. There is an abundant supply that cannot run out. It is free and available to every rider in the world, but some never receive Christ. Some decide they don't need Him. Still others taste and see, but let other things crowd out the importance of it and leave it behind. Thankfully, some see, take, enjoy, and keep the salvation that is available to every man and woman. It was there for all, for the taking.

A Free House

My father bought a farm in Iowa near the other farms my family owned and operated. This farm had a high hill covered with a grove of trees. We had rented it for many years, so I knew the area well. The large grove was a great place to hunt squirrel, turkey, and deer. We often used it on Christmas vacations to hunt together as a family. As little tykes, my sons carried their first guns across its rolling landscape amidst the trees and meadows. Our cattle roamed through its woods on windy days to avoid the chill that blew across the prairie in the winters.

After my father purchased the farm, I walked the timberland with him squirrel hunting on a beautiful fall day in October. We arrived at my favorite place, a clearing in the woods on the back side at the highest point on the entire farm. From there, we could see the main farmstead where my brother now lived, some four miles across the open fields. Off to the left, the grain towers of my hometown broke the horizon. Off to the right, the rolling hills covered with the grandeur of the crops near harvest time almost covered the grain elevators of the little village that had always been our closest connection to civilization.

As we stood there enjoying the Iowa beauty ("Iowa" is an Indian word meaning "beautiful land"), I told my dad I wanted to build a house for him right there. I told him I would build it and pay for it. I could have the plans drawn over the winter, break ground in February, and have him in it by Thanksgiving next year. He could have a new, larger house out in the country rather than the small house in town where he had retired.

I had built four homes, all my own personal residences, in various parts of the country. They were fine, upscale homes that he knew well were a cut above. Nothing was average about them. My offer was good.

He turned it down. He said he did not want a new house; he was happy with the small home he had. Well, it was his choice. You can't make someone take something if they don't want it. The discussion of the possibility of a new house stopped dead in it tracks right there. I was forty-one; my father was in his sixties. I knew him well enough not to argue or try to persuade him. Once he declared his decision, it was time to move on to the next topic.

Salvation is like that. The offer for a home in heaven is given to you and every single person on the planet. It is paid for and available. All you must do is say, "Yes, I'll take it." It's yours. But you can turn it down. No one will force you to take it. You can continue to live on the wrong side of heaven, but you will never be able to say you didn't have a heavenly home available for the taking. Jesus died for every single soul on the earth. All they must do is say, "Yes, I take Jesus." No one will ever be able to charge God with unfairness that He provided for some and not for others. Jesus paid it all for everyone. But not everyone will take what He has given.

Romans 1:20 (GW)

From the creation of the world, God's invisible qualities,

his eternal power and divine nature,

have been clearly observed in what he made.

As a result, people have no excuse.

CHAPTER 16

LIFE'S FINAL LESSON

Ecclesiastes 8:8

There is no man that hath power over the spirit to
retain the spirit;
neither hath he power in the day of death:
and there is no discharge in that war . . .

Late-Breaking News

In a dense fog on I-40 outside of Albuquerque, New Mexico, eight people die instantly as a van crashes into the back of a truck that had stopped on the roadway. At the central hospital in downtown Santa Fe, an elderly man slips into a coma and takes his last breath. In a back alley in Chicago, a teen is shot to death by a drug addict who wanted his wristwatch so he could buy more drugs. On the tenth floor of a Manhattan high-rise, a man passes away as his heart fails under the stress of the day.

All that happened in a single second. At the time of the writing of this book, there are four and one-third births per second. Within the space of approximately 125 years, every one of those people will have died. That means the death rate is equal to the birth rate, one apiece. With the current population of the planet at 7.5 billion people, within 125 years, 7.5 billion people will die unless God intervenes.

Before I knew Christ, I never gave death much thought. I was too young and bulletproof to see much imminent danger in it. After becoming a Christian, eternity became a topic I thought a lot about. And getting to eternity, unless God finds another way, meant passing through death. We know there is life on the other side of death by the hope and faith we have in God's promises. We even have hope in alternative ways to eternity, like the concept of a rapture mentioned by the apostle Paul (1 Thessalonians 4:17).

Shadows across the Tombstones

As a young missionary pastor, I held far too many funerals. Many were for unchurched families who came to me after the fact, wanting someone to read scripture and say some kind words over a departed loved one. No matter whom the person was or the circumstances, I had this deep-seated anguish that death was too harsh of a punishment for mankind. Had God been too angry when He imposed such a drastic punishment on man for the rebellion and disobedience he had committed?

It was four o'clock in the afternoon and the shadows were lengthening. I had taken the day off to walk and reflect after an exhausting Sunday full of services and activity. I drove into the countryside and found a place to be alone. Among my favorite stops were cemeteries. They were quiet, peaceful, and full of history. As I walked through them, I read the grave markers, noticed the dates, and pondered the importance of the last phrase on their markers.

I was in southeastern Illinois where the prairie begins and spreads to the north and west for two thousand miles. I had ventured across an older cemetery with dates much older than those on the western prairie. The area had been settled long before the great migration to the westward lands. The dates on the tombstones were from years absent from those on the western prairie. The trees had grown large and numerous so that the whole area was dark and shaded more than the open-sky cemeteries west of the Mississippi River.

The cool shade darkened the rows of stone monuments and brought a mysterious silence over the scene. I lifted my eyes from the nearby stones to gaze across row after row of tombstones. The sight closed in on me with an overwhelming sadness. Tears came to my eyes as I traveled in my mind through the lives of so many decades of time; there was so much death.

I looked up through the branches to the heavens and silently uttered a prayerful question to God, "Why didn't you bring Adam here so he could see this death and destruction?"

There was silence. No voice answered.

"If only Adam could have seen this place, he would not have resolved to betray You!"

The heavens were silent.

It is just like God to give answers with a still, small voice. He could shout it, thunder it, write in the sky, or burn it into a rock and drop it on my head. But He was gentle and kind to this young wayfarer who had come to challenge Him, just as Adam must have done on that fateful day. Oh, how we question God and impugn His integrity!

As my eyes cleared and I once again gazed across the rows of stones, the answer came: "I told him. And even if he had come here, it would not have changed anything."

Oh, the lesson He taught me that day. Through the centuries, He seeks out those who will believe and trust just His word. Thomas had to hear and see to believe Jesus had risen. John recorded the reaction from Jesus about Thomas's hesitation to accept the words of testimony given him in John 20:29: "Blessed are they that have not seen, and yet have believed."

God is honored by those who believe and follow. It is not the brilliant and scholarly, not the high and exalted, but the simple who just believe. If Adam had just believed what God had told him, history would have been different. Who was I to question the judgment of God or the care He took in teaching Adam?

Mankind has trouble simply accepting God at his word. How insulting that is to God. At the sound of His voice, the world was created out of nothing. At the sound of His voice, light was created and shined in the heavens. God spoke and all of creation took notice and obeyed His command. But mankind does not respond to the voice of God in the same way. We fail to take Him at His word. We fail to believe.

Humans think they are gods in their own right and can question God. It is a heart issue; it is a wanting to be God or thinking we are equal to God. When all of creation hears and obeys the voice of God and we are the only creatures that don't, what does that make us? Who am I to question Him?

The Perfect Punishment

Death is the perfect punishment for the thief who attempts to take everything and refuses to stop his adventurous rampage. Death makes the thief give back what he has taken. And since the thief will not give up the quest to own, death is the final solution. Death makes you give up everything, including your life. Death was the only fitting solution and punishment for stealing God's kingdom, power, and glory.

There have been criminals who stole vast amounts of wealth and took their punishment for years in prison, all the while keeping the money hidden so they could get it once released. God is not so foolish as to leave that option. God takes back what is His and does not give the opportunity to the thief to enjoy the fruits of his crime.

Ecclesiastes 8:8 concludes that we do not have the power in our final day to lengthen our life. The verse reads, "There is no man that hath power over the spirit to retain the spirit; neither hath he power in the day of death: and there is no discharge in that war." It is above our pay grade. Life is beyond our ability to preserve it. We must admit that there is a power above us on that day that we cannot defeat or outwit. On the day we die, we learn a lesson that we should have learned earlier.

God is the ultimate owner and has been all along. Living under His ownership would have made life better while we had time to enjoy it and reap its peace and rest. We learn God's ownership extends to the full ability to terminate us on the day He calls our number. It is far better to learn now, while you still can enjoy His care and decide in this present life to live under God's ownership. God has given us the opportunity to walk with Him in the cool of the day in the Garden just as Adam did. We have been given a place characterized by rest and peace. It is there just for the taking.

The Last Lesson You Learn

If you haven't discovered it by then, the last lesson you will learn on the day you die is that God is the owner. He has been the owner all the time, even though you thought on some days you had it all in your pocket—it was not real. You fooled yourself and the rest of the world, but not God.

If you have stolen this earth, you can't keep it. You must give it back. He may let you use it, but He won't give it to you. You may think you will own a burial plot here and have the last laugh owning a little piece, but although the pyramid tombs in Egypt have lasted a long time, they are empty of any owner who may have thought he would keep something.

How foolish we are to think we could have owned the planet. We don't have the power to make it rain, cool or heat it, nor to keep it spinning. It takes an all-powerful God to be able to own this magnificent creation.

Rejoice with me as we proclaim our great God has the whole world in His hands. He always has and always will.

Matthew 6:13

For thine is the kingdom, and the power,
and the glory, for ever. Amen.

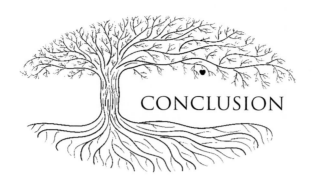

CONCLUSION

THE MYSTERY
OF GOD REVEALED

Revelation 10:7, 10 (ESV)

The mystery of God
would be fulfilled,
just as he announced to his servants the prophets.

And I took the little scroll from the hand of the angel and ate it.
It was sweet as honey in my mouth,
but when I had eaten it my stomach was made bitter.

The mystery of God mentioned in Revelation 10:7 will always be open to interpretation. Every Bible student may well have his or her own view as to the meaning of that mystery. It is no mystery to God. The mystery is a dilemma only for mankind. We are in the dark and are unable to determine the nature of who God is or what He looks like, assuming He will be visible aside from the physical presence of Jesus. We are limited by time, space, and physical dimensions. How can we comprehend a being that has no limits as we know them? We are unable to comprehend what is beyond space, without matter, and not bound by time. Being God is something ONLY He can know until we come into His presence.

Having spent fifty years pursuing Jesus and the Father who sent Him, I have come to understand the mystery of God as He has revealed it to me. That is not to say that I know something others don't. It is simply my perspective from the journey God led me through. As I see the mystery from my point of view, I believe it is the simple fact of God's ownership.

The mystery of His ownership exists because we don't want to see it. It is our root sin. Just as Adam hid in the Garden, denied, and blamed, so we continue that same pattern. God has chosen to hide it so that only those who really want to follow will be able to find it. He could have painted it in the sky in large letters so none could miss it. He could have killed Adam and Eve instantly and enforced his ownership. But He chooses to seek out those who would seek Him *until they find Him.*

Deuteronomy 4:29 (ESV)

But from there you will seek the LORD your God
and you will find him,
if you search after him with all your heart and all your soul.

I believe the scroll mentioned in Revelation 10:10 is a deed of ownership to all God has created. It may be written in a general nature. A deed that mentions every human who ever lived would require a few billion pages at least. However, if the deed were a general deed for Adam written to include his offspring, then a single paragraph would handle humanity. Another paragraph to accommodate the title to earth and the other matter in the universe, along with a phrase encumbering the space, would take care of all that we are conscious of existing. Throw in a sentence for the intangibles such as time and gravity as he invented them. The scroll could easily be as small as He portrayed the work of creation in a chapter or two of Genesis.

John is told to eat the scroll. I think that means to devour it mentally. And when he does, it is sweet at first, but sour later when John realizes the full meaning. We can easily be happy about some news until we realize the implications and the trouble that follows on the heels of that information. It may sound great at first, but then we must deal with the fallout.

I think John's first impression was ecstasy. It was so simple to him. The fact that God owned the universe and every single person on the planet was easy information to assimilate. John was saying to himself, "If that is all there is, God, we can handle this. We got it, we will get on board right away. Thank God the mystery was not some complicated thing that was impossible for us to do. Sweet! God's great mystery is simple."

But then, John had an epiphany: If it was that simple, why have we not done it? Why have we not given God ownership of all He created?

John realized that the heart of man was so greedy and evil, only God's force—even into the future—would be required to impose God's ownership. He realized the great failure of every man all the way through history. Only a few had found the truth, and even they battled every single day against the flesh to try to honor His ownership.

Being God is our sin.

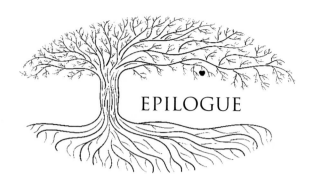

EPILOGUE

We have a choice. God gives us free will. We are not robots; we can choose to take the apple and own ourselves, or we can submit to His ownership. As we recognize and live under His authority as owner, we will daily face the temptation to take back possession of situations and events, because we were born with that inclination. We will never escape our humanity that leads us into temptation until the resurrection of the next life perfects us. Until then, we can rejoice in knowing the true battle we face having now discovered the depth of our human fault line. Now we can see the true nature of how we offend God daily by being God.

I enjoy living in the Promised Land, God's rest. But the moment I take ownership of a problem, I have a ticket to the wilderness level. As long as we are in this body on this side of heaven, we are tenants, not owners, and will struggle against our own humanity to stay in the Place of Rest. We are our own worst enemy. It is only our own desires that take us out of the Place of Rest.

James 1:14

But every man is tempted,
when he is drawn away of his own lust, and enticed.

Make no mistake; no one can destroy our life and peace more than we ourselves. No person has the power you have over your destiny, to live under God's authority, or throw yourself into the fury and fire of self-exalting. There is that ever-present human tendency to pick up something that belongs to God.

The author has not centered this work on pride or humility. But in exalting God back to His original state as the authority derived from His ownership, it is clear that the sin of man is much deeper than we had considered before. We have been far too easy on mankind, thinking we just had a few behavior problems to confess and correct. The true nature of our sin is buried deep in our hearts. There is no room for pride at any level of Christianity. Our thieving nature brings us to our knees each hour to confess we are far below the authority and holiness of our true God. The truth of who He is will drive us to our knees.

This is not an exhaustive study. I have only introduced the topic to you and laid out some areas to consider. There is no end to the ways and means that man has devised to be his own God. I challenge you to go beyond and discover more that will take you to the mountaintops in your relationship with God.

Don't stop here; go on to have the best relationship you can with the creator who loves you dearly. I challenge you to write an even better, more in-depth book on the topic of man's basic sin, Being God.

WHO WILL BE YOUR GOD?

NOTE FROM THE AUTHOR

The intent of this book is to start you on the greatest quest of your life, to find the Abundant Life by learning your true relationship with God as your owner. It is my attempt to be brief with what I view as the greatest topic of the universe. I pray and hope this will start you on a lifelong journey to discover the truth of who you are and what your correct relationship with God should be.

I have structured the book on the premise that you are already a Christian and have a relationship with Jesus as your Savior. No attempt has been made to persuade unbelievers to connect with Jesus within the manuscript of the book. I do believe lifting God to the highest position possible will open the door to the love that God has displayed in giving to us the magnificent gift of Jesus's sacrifice on the cross for the payment of our sins.

John 3:16

For God so loved the world,

that he gave his only begotten Son,

that whosoever believeth in him should not perish,

but have everlasting life.

If you are not a follower of Jesus, or do not *know* that you are bound for heaven, the following prayer will get you connected to Jesus, the only provider of the means to attain heaven:

> Almighty God and Father in Heaven, forgive me of my sin. I confess that I have been the owner of my life and have lived apart from God in rebellion against your love. I have committed sins as I have been on my own journey traveling away from God. Thank you for loving me and providing the shed blood of Jesus to pay for my sin. I accept Jesus and His death on the cross as payment for my sins and declare Jesus to be my Savior. Amen.

Read your Bible. Begin in the Gospels of Mark and John. Contact a local church for further help. Write the author on his website at www.BeingGod.org for assistance.

1 John 5:11–13

And this is the record, that God hath given to us

eternal life,

and this life is in his Son.

He that hath the Son hath life;

and he that hath not the Son of God hath not life.
These things have I written unto you that believe on
the name of the Son of God;
that ye may know that ye have eternal life,
and that ye may believe on the name of the Son of God.

LEADER'S GUIDE

QUESTIONS
FOR DISCUSSION

Introduction:

1. Give your evaluation of Isaiah 2:11.

2. Convey some of your meditations and thoughts on the last phrase of the Lord's Prayer.

3. Describe how you take care of the things you own.

4. How would you describe your life if someone owned you?

5. What would your life be like if you lived as though God owned you?

6. Describe ways in which you have owned the Kingdom.

7. Describe ways you may have owned God's power.

8. Describe ways you may have owned God's glory.

Chapter 1: Three Words That Changed My Life Forever

1. Relate a time when you were the answer to someone's prayer.

2. List giant requests you have made from God for you to help others.

3. Describe an incident in which you were used to verbally give the Gospel.

4. Compare your travels for pleasure to the Lord's journeys He sent you on.

5. List people who will smile and greet you in heaven and thank you.

6. What phrase or question can you use to start a spiritual conversation?

Chapter 2: Ownership

1. Give your evaluation of Malachi 3:8.

2. Tell us about something you owned that you regretted owning.

3. Tell us about something you owned that you may have had success with.

4. Can you give some examples of items or areas of your life you would like God to own?

5. Can you give examples of areas of your life God owned?

6. Give your thoughts on Jeremiah 17:9.

Chapter 3: Burnout and Midlife Crisis

1. Define "burnout" and compare it to "midlife crisis."

2. What expectations have you had that were unrealistic?

3. What would your relationships be like if you listened twice as much as you spoke?

4. Describe times you felt alone or were carrying the entire load with no help.

5. Detail things you can do to share the load equally.

6. Describe the times you thought you were the driver instead of under the yoke.

Chapter 4: Living under His Ownership

1. Describe situations that you handled without God that did not go well.

2. Describe a situation or incident that you refused to own and God had to solve.

3. List changes that have occurred in your life because of following Jesus.

4. How have you changed in personality and temperament?

5. What change was not permanent that still needs attention?

6. List those you still need to forgive.

Chapter 5: Bird's-Eye View

1. Describe what it's like to be lost.

2. Describe a travel experience to a place where you could not read the road signs.

3. Give your feelings in a major move or cultural change.

4. Give an overall view of the Bible on sin, salvation, man, and angels.

5. Narrow down to one character in the Bible like you and elaborate.

6. Describe how that character fits into the overall Bible narrative.

Chapter 6: The View from Heaven

1. Share your thought on Lamentations 1:12.

2. If you have ever been robbed, tell us how you felt after it happened.

3. Tell us how you feel when something is missing.

4. Tell us about a loss you have suffered and the feelings and impact it had on you.

5. Try to imagine and put in words how God might have felt at the loss of Adam and Eve.

6. Describe your feelings and thought when you have lost intangibles such as dignity and respect.

Chapter 7: New Testament Promised Land—The Place of Rest

1. What spiritual goal did you have before you read this chapter?

2. Explain a situation or event you let God own and solve for you.

3. Give examples of events or situations you have owned and tried to solve.

4. Describe how living in the Place of Rest would make you a different person.

5. Have you considered the length of your life and how you will face death?

6. What have you learned from some hard-won lessons?

Chapter 8: Lost in Translation

1. Compare your two favorite Bible versions.

2. Give your explanation of how you previously defined the word "Lord."

3. What topics or doctrines are you willing to wait for Jesus to clarify for you later?

4. How much have you given thought previously to God's ownership?

5. Why is it hard for us to use other versions than the Authorized King James Version?

6. How much have language and definitions changed in your lifetime so far?

Chapter 9: The Discovery

1. What truths have you discovered in the Bible that were life changing or profound?

2. Describe a problem or situation you let God own and solve for you.

3. What have you considered to be the Abundant Life in your view?

4. Describe an area or problem in your past life that God helped you win the victory over.

5. What evidence do you have that you may be carrying hidden baggage?

6. List some debts or baggage from the past that has not been solved or forgiven.

Chapter 10: Two Levels of Christian Life

1. What perspective do you have about the Christian life?

2. What milestones have you reached in your journey to maturity?

3. Compare the work and value to Jesus of paid staff and unpaid volunteers.

4. Describe a time you had perfect peace.

5. Describe peace.

6. Compare Jonah's two directions to different times in your life.

Chapter 11: In the Beginning—The Garden of Eden

1. How have you viewed the events that transpired in the Garden of Eden up to this time?

2. List changes you may have had in your view after reading this chapter.

3. List the things Adam and Eve did incorrectly in your view.

4. Describe how you think Adam and Eve may have thought that caused their bad choices.

5. Relate your experiences with the word "mine."

6. What are the first words your children learned on their own?

Chapter 12: The Garden Crime Scene Investigation

1. Describe the events and attitude displayed by Lucifer in Isaiah 14:12–14.

2. How would you evaluate the punishments set forth to Adam and Eve from God?

3. How deep do you view yourself in ongoing efforts to control or own your situation?

4. Evaluate the level man lifts himself to at equal with God or above God and tell us why.

5. How does the prospect of physical death affect you?

6. Evaluate the different effects of spiritual and mental (soul) death on you.

Chapter 13: Journey through the Wilderness

1. What lessons or applications did you make in the past about the wilderness journey?

2. Where are you on the spiritual journey as it relates to the map of their journey?

3. What do you think the Place of Rest will be like?

4. Describe a trip you made where the journey was more difficult than it should have been.

5. Where in the journey are people locked into doctrinal detail and correctness?

6. Explain how unbelief can keep us from God's best.

Chapter 14: Foundations in Scripture

1. Meditate slowly on the Lord's Prayer and give insights you discover.

2. Relate what it means to be an owner of something.

3. Name something you thought you had given to God.

4. Compare your size and importance to the billboard of space and stars.

5. Describe the relationship of a shepherd to sheep.

6. Evaluate the price God paid to bring you back to Him.

Chapter 15: Text Message from Heaven

1. What proof do you have of the resurrection?

2. What proof do you have that Jesus forgave you (hint: 1 John 5:11–13)?

3. Describe how you came to be a follower of Jesus.

4. What internal things hold you back from being a total, committed follower of Jesus?

5. What things of this world stand in your way of following?

6. What doctrines do you hold more sacred than following?

Chapter 16: Life's Final Lesson

1. What plans have you made for later in life?

2. What plans have you made in case you don't make it to later in life?

3. Compare a car making plans as opposed to its owner making plans.

4. What things do you still question God about?

5. How do you view death?

6. Ponder your last days and contemplate whether you will have panic or peace, and why.

Conclusion: The Mystery of God Revealed

1. Do a Bible search on the eleven mysteries listed in the Bible.

2. List the years or seasons of your life you were closest to God.

3. Describe how keeping His ownership in mind could make Christian life easy.

4. Compare the issue of His ownership to other disciplines you endeavor to master.

5. Elaborate about how new this concept is to you.

6. List ways you will put this truth to work to bring peace to your life.

ABOUT THE AUTHOR

Terry Stueck is a missionary, author, and speaker. His book detailing unconditional forgiveness, *Forgive Instantly & Live Free*, is rated five stars and is used internationally as a curriculum aid for Gospel Rescue Missions, marriage counseling, divorce recovery, and church study groups. He is a graduate of Missouri State University and Faith Theological Seminary. He began inner-city mission work at the Bible Rescue  Mission in the heart of Chicago's infamous "Skid Row" and the Pacific Garden Mission on Chicago's South Side. His missionary service extends from inner cities, church planting, church rescue, military-installation communities, and prison ministry. In 1997, he founded High Plains Bible Mission in New Mexico as an outreach to native and inner-city communities. He currently serves as mission director.

OTHER BOOKS BY TERRY STUEK

FORGIVE
INSTANTLY & LIVE FREE

Master the art of forgiving instantly.
Find the mysterious key to the Abundant Life.
Learn how to correctly forgive and set yourself free from
anger, stress, hang-ups, and addictions.

Forgiveness is the bottom line of Christianity. All want
forgiveness from others and God, but few learn the benefit that

forgiving brings to the heart and soul. The author explains how to free one's life to live abundantly by learning both components of forgiving. He then takes the reader to new heights in the Christian walk by giving the reader the door to a new perspective that allows one to be instantly forgiving.

Improve your ability to "let go" by learning the second component of forgiving.

Explore a new deeper relationship with God as "owner" of your problems.

Cure Anger—Don't manage it.

Wipe out Stress—Don't live with it.

Defeat addictions—Don't tolerate them.

Grow your Faith—Don't settle for mediocrity.

Find True Happiness—Don't waste your life.

How to Have Real Change in Your Life

Available at www.forgiveinstantly.com and Amazon paperback, hardcover, eBook, and Audible.